50 SUCCESSFUL HARVARD MEDICAL SCHOOL ESSAYS

T0054513

Also by the Staff of *The Harvard Crimson*

50 Successful Harvard Application Essays: Editions 1–5
55 Successful Harvard Law School Application Essays:
Editions 1 and 2
How They Got into Harvard

50
SUCCESSFUL
HARVARD
MEDICAL
SCHOOL
ESSAYS

With Analysis by the Staff of *The Harvard Crimson*

ST. MARTIN'S GRIFFIN
NEW YORK

First published in the United States by St. Martin's Griffin, an imprint of St. Martin's Publishing Group

50 SUCCESSFUL HARVARD MEDICAL SCHOOL ESSAYS. Copyright © 2020 by *The Harvard Crimson*. All rights reserved. Printed in the United States of America. For information, address St. Martin's Publishing Group, 120 Broadway, New York, NY 10271.

www.stmartins.com

Library of Congress Cataloging-in-Publication Data

Title: 50 successful Harvard Medical School essays / with analysis by the Staff of the Harvard Crimson.
Other titles: Fifty successful Harvard Medical School essays | Harvard crimson.
Description: First St. Martin's Griffin edition. | New York : St. Martin's Griffin, 2020.
Identifiers: LCCN 2019058372 | ISBN 9781250244475 (trade paperback) | ISBN 9781250244482 (ebook)
Subjects: LCSH: Harvard Medical School—Admission. | Medical colleges—United States—Admission. | Medical colleges—Massachusetts—Boston. | Essays. | Exposition (Rhetoric) | College applications—Massachusetts—Boston.
Classification: LCC R838.4 .A17 2020 | DDC 610.71/174461—dc23
LC record available at https://lccn.loc.gov/2019058372

Our books may be purchased in bulk for promotional, educational, or business use. Please contact your local bookseller or the Macmillan Corporate and Premium Sales Department at 1-800-221-7945, extension 5442, or by email at MacmillanSpecialMarkets@macmillan.com.

First Edition: May 2020

D 10 9 8 7 6 5 4 3 2

CONTENTS

Acknowledgments   ix
Introduction   xi

I. PASSION

Jun Liu   3
Zachary Johannesson   7
Jacqueline Boehme   11
Andrew Maul   15
Jonathan Fisher   19
Lashyra "Lash" Nolen   23
Emily Rencsok   27
Agatha Brzezinski   31
Perry Choi   35
Ryan Bartholomew   39
Keizra Mecklai   43
A.S.   48
Nina Allen   52
Eileen O'Callaghan   56
Johnathan Weslow   60

II. INFLUENTIAL FIGURE

Derek Soled   67
Logan Carter   71
Hazel W.   75

Contents

Brian Yang   79

Gregory Haman   83

Kyle R. B.   87

Michael Wu   91

Megha Majumder   95

III. IMPACTFUL EXPERIENCE

Ashley Shaw   101

Marissa Lynn   105

Omar Abudayyeh   109

Selena Li   113

Jane Miller   117

Emma Meyers   121

Larisa Shagabayeva   125

Katherine Redfield   129

Felicia H.   134

Melody King   138

Amy Martin   142

Travis Benson   146

Gabriel Molina   151

IV. IDENTITY

Robert Weatherford   159

Azucena Ramos   163

Sergio G. Núñez Báez   168

Kobby A.   172

Grant Schleifer   177

Francisco Ramos   181

Gregory Peters   185

Contents

Christopher Huenneke   189
Manuela von Sneidern   193

V. INTELLECTUAL DESIRE

Aurelia Lee   199
Angela Castellanos   203
Jennifer Choi   208
Kate Koch   212
J. C. Panagides   216

Applicant Advice   221

ACKNOWLEDGMENTS

I would first like to thank our amazing editors at St. Martin's Press, Laura Apperson and Sallie Lotz, for believing in the first book of this new series and for providing us with endless support and guidance as we compiled the book. I would also like to express my sincerest gratitude to the fifty contributing medical students. Thank you for sharing your stories and wisdom with aspiring students all around the world; this book would not be possible without your commitment and dedication to supporting the next generation of doctors. Last but certainly not least, thank you to members of the *Crimson* staff whose perseverance and passion for this book made it a success. In no particular order, thank you to Katharina Wolf, Owen Searle, George Moe, Melissa Du, Evelyn Manyatta, Deni Hoxha, and Rebecca Lisk. We did it.

—Sabrina W. Chok
Publishing Manager,
146th Guard of *The Harvard Crimson*

INTRODUCTION

Competition for admittance into the nation's top medical schools has never been more intense and it has become increasingly important to write a personal statement that sets you apart from thousands of other medical school applicants.

However, that is a daunting task—in less than fifty-three hundred characters, you must weave together your experiences, interests, and passions into a memorable and evocative narrative that resonates with a panel of admissions officers. While there is no magic formula for writing the perfect essay, by picking up this helpful book you are already on the right track. Whether you are just beginning to write your essay or have written several drafts already, this book will provide you with the insights and guidance you need to succeed.

On these next pages, you will find fifty standout essays that helped students successfully secure a spot at Harvard Medical School, one of the best medical schools in the country. No two essays are the same: A young woman describes creating mental health awareness in her community. A hockey player opens up about their unexpected entrance into sports medicine. A pianist explores the intersection between music and care. Each student presents a different set of experiences, ideas, and perspectives that informs their path to medicine.

Each essay is coupled with analysis by a *Crimson* editor or editors on specific essay qualities and techniques that worked, so you can learn from their example and apply it to your own writing.

Introduction

You will find that for many of these essays, their strengths lie not in the writer's topic of choice, but instead, in the writer's ability to forward an argument about their character, drive, and passion for medicine with elegant prose, precise organization, and sometimes even a sprinkle of unexpectedly charming humor.

We have divided the book into five thematic categories: Passion, Influential Figure, Impactful Experience, Identity, and Intellectual Desire. While these broad themes by no means fully encapsulate the complexity and depth of each of these essays, we hope they will serve as helpful guiding points as you pinpoint the types of stories you want to tell. At the end of this book, you will find a chapter filled with words of wisdom from some of the students behind these essays. We hope their words will encourage and guide you as you embark on this journey.

We wish you the best of luck with writing your essay and finding the medical school that is right for you.

—Sabrina W. Chok
Publishing Manager,
146th Guard of *The Harvard Crimson*

I. PASSION

JUN LIU

Hometown: Nanjing, China
Undergraduate School: Private, Williams College
Major: Biology
GPA: 3.86
MCAT: 36. PS: 10, V: 14, BS: 12.

ESSAY

Detention. The word filled me with youthful indignation. I knew I was being punished for tasting the alkali earth metal salts we were categorizing in the science lab, but from my 12-year-old's perspective, I was in legendary company. My hero, Dr. Shizhen Li, the 16th century Chinese herbalist from my history books, had famously risked his own health to locate and sample the thousands of medicines he exhaustively researched for his Compendium of Materia Medica. Though the punishment tempered my reckless tasting of lab materials, it failed to restrain my adventurous spirit. Like the relentless Dr. Li, my aspirations to become a physician-scientist have spanned the globe and led to unexpected journeys.

In my early years, two very important women inspired me to carefully question conventional wisdom. My grandmother was obsessed with the medicinal properties of food. Diagnosed with severe diabetes in her 70s, she ignored her physician's advice to begin insulin shots and successfully controlled her condition with diet and exercise. As a child, I eagerly followed her maverick example. I must have seemed an earnest little quack, "prescribing" all kinds of foods to "cure" my friends' ailments. But it wasn't simply play. I still find myself resorting to some of my grandmother's herbal solutions. I even converted my undergraduate thesis advisor into the habit of drinking Chinese Tieguanyin tea to fight his Coca-Cola "addiction."

My close relationship with my grandmother prompted an early interest in nutrition and natural remedies. But it was my admiration for my mother's work as a leading HIV/STD epidemiologist for China's CDC that introduced me to the essential roles of public outreach and research in battling diseases. As a teen, I took on the tasks of performing simple data analysis in my mother's lab and distributing handouts from the CDC detailing STD support resources in clinics. I particularly enjoyed face-to-face interaction with patients, and was intrigued by the close collaboration between doctors and epidemiologists. Moreover, I began to understand the stake we have in overcoming cultural taboos in order to prevent, detect and treat infectious diseases. Talking with young AIDS patients fighting uphill battles, I realized I didn't have the patience to wait until I received a physician's license to spread the "gospel" of preventive care. I felt compelled to act.

Recognizing that a Chinese medical education would focus almost exclusively on the hard sciences, I decided to instead pursue a US liberal arts education despite considerable obstacles. I yearned for the freedom to engage with the public to promote disease prevention and explore the diversity of factors affecting health. Williams College offered me the opportunity to connect my passion for medical science with my concern for the community through the student organization Public Health Alliance. First as a participant, and then as Chair, I worked with campus and community leaders to raise awareness of preventable and sometimes controversial health issues since my sophomore year—ranging from sports injuries to HPV awareness—facing the Williams community. My undergraduate years also sparked my love for the interdisciplinary nature of neuroscience and deepened my interest in research. Rewarding laboratory experience, clinical shadowing, and mentorship from physician-scientists reinforced my aspiration to work at the exciting interface between brain research and medicine.

After graduation, winning the Herchel Smith Fellowship allowed me to embark on another journey to the University of Cambridge, UK. I enjoyed in-depth research training in the lab of Prof. Andrea Brand, who pioneers in genetic strategies to study neural stem cell (NSC) regulation. I believe that understanding fundamental mechanisms in this field will be key to preventing and curing many fatal CNS diseases, such as certain types of neurodegenerative disorders and brain tumors. My PhD research investigates mechanisms of amino acid regulation of NSCs, which enabled me to unite my earlier interests in nutrition and the brain. Outside the lab, I sought to understand neuronal diseases from both the doctor's and patient's perspective by shadowing neuroradiologists and volunteering at a dementia care center. The exposure to laboratory and clinical neuroscience in the past 2.5 years has motivated me to continue investigating NSC biology as a physician-scientist.

With the aid of a comprehensive medical training, I am eager to extend my current interest in nutritional control of NSCs to improving brain care. Understanding the regulation of NSCs on a molecular level will help me to develop targeted approaches for interventional therapies. When screening for potential therapeutics, I am particularly interested in expanding the current range of available synthetic compounds to naturally occurring ones derived from plant extracts. Ultimately, I hope to contribute to the prevention and treatment of neuronal diseases by developing novel therapies that will benefit patients.

ANALYSIS

From the start of the essay, it is clear that Jun is a natural story-teller and this aids him when sharing a compelling narrative of his aspirations towards becoming a physician-scientist. Whether it's phrases like "legendary company" from his introductory anecdote in which he perfectly conveys the sense of triumph his twelve-year-old self felt after landing himself in detention or the way he describes himself as an "earnest little quack," Jun skillfully adds snippets of his personality and witty humor into his essay. He uses specificity and imagery to his advantage, employing telling examples that show readers the experiences that not only connect him to medicine but also convey his curious and defiant nature. In doing so, he successfully keeps his readers engaged as he transitions into the second half of his essay, where he details his medicine-motivated journey around the world.

Though he pivots to a less playful style of writing in the latter half of his essay, he is able to elegantly weave together his collective experiences into a coherent narrative. With each experience, more than simply exploring the nuances behind the impact it had on him, he describes how it compelled him to take action and to further his relationship with medicine. By the conclusion of his essay, he demonstrates his ability to be a passionate and proactive learner through highly specific examples and successfully leaves readers with a clear idea of his character and aspirations.

—Sabrina Chok

ZACHARY JOHANNESSON

Hometown: Peterborough, New Hampshire, USA
Undergraduate School: Public, University of North Carolina
  at Wilmington
Major: Biology
GPA: 4.0
MCAT: 510. CP: 126, CARS: 131, BB: 127, PS: 126.

ESSAY

When I first joined the Marines at 17, I wanted to "fight for freedom" and give back to my country. I joined the infantry because I wanted to be where the fight was, and that was the surest way to end up in Iraq or Afghanistan. Three years later, I finally found myself in Afghanistan, leading a 3-man fire team. When I first arrived in May 2011, I felt as if we were going to make the region, if not the whole world, a better place by removing some of the evil from it. My experience over the next 7 months, however, proved to be more nuanced than anticipated.

When I arrived in Marjah, almost a year after the initial invasion to oust the Taliban from the city, most of the large-scale fighting had ceased. Most of the "good" I thought I would be doing had already been done, and the Taliban that survived had either fled or hid among the populace using guerrilla tactics. The city was in the early stages of rebuilding and a sense of normalcy had returned. Over the course of my deployment, we helped facilitate the reconstruction of the city while fighting off the occasional Taliban attack.

What ended up remaining with me after my return from

Afghanistan was not the good we did by removing the Taliban, but rather the good we were able to do by taking small actions to help the locals. This ranged from actions as simple as providing locals with water, to actions as complex as rendering medical care to those in need. While I never actively participated in providing treatment to locals, I was struck by how large an impact these treatments could have on an individual. In one particular instance, while on patrol, I was approached by a man who had been kicked by his cow and had a severe infection on his arm. Most of the flesh surrounding his wound was inflamed and red, and he was in excruciating pain. My corpsman came up to the man, instructing him to come by our patrol base later for treatment, and his infection was eventually cleared. Having spent the majority of my life in the United States, I had always taken modern medicine, particularly antibiotics, for granted. In Afghanistan, however, where there was little to no access to modern medicine, I was able to appreciate just how beneficial it truly is.

When I got out of the military the following summer and prepared to attend college, I wanted to continue to be in a career where I was able to benefit others. My experience in Afghanistan, witnessing the power of medicine, combined with the interest I gained in medicine following my trauma training, drove me towards health care. I entered Cape Fear Community College with the intention of joining their highly competitive nursing program. My first semester consisted of mostly electives in addition to Anatomy & Physiology, a class I had previously considered too hard. I was completely fascinated by the material and, following completion of the class, wanted to learn more. This captivation continued as I progressed through my science classes.

I became fascinated in infectious disease following a class in microbiology. After completion of the course, I continued to pursue the subject outside of class, reading several books on various infectious diseases. This interest prompted me to transfer to UNCW, instead of continuing into the nursing program, where I could continue to study the subject more in-depth. While at UNCW, the majority of my biology coursework, as well as my two research projects, focused on infectious diseases, cementing my interest in the subject. While I briefly considered pursuing a PhD in microbiology, my desire to work closely with, and treat, patients led me to apply to medical school. My time shadowing at Wilmington Health reinforced my decision to apply to medical school.

Following medical school, I intend on training in an infectious disease fellowship, where I will be able to combine my interest in microbiology with my desire to help others. I contemplated applying for MD/PhD programs to enable me to research, while still being able to interact with patients. I decided, however, to apply to MD only programs, wanting the majority of my focus to be on one on one patient care.

While I am certainly interested in practicing medicine within the United States, after completion of my training I am also highly interested in working with an organization like Doctors Without Borders, enabling me to once again be part of a team bringing healthcare to underserved individuals around the globe. After my experience in Afghanistan, and making the decision to work in medicine, this is an opportunity I've been highly interested in, particularly with my desire to work in infectious disease, as many of the regions this organization operates in are still burdened by endemic diseases, such as tuberculosis and malaria, as well as emerging diseases, such as Ebola.

For the aforementioned reasons, I would like to attend medical school and pursue a career in medicine. It is a career where I'm achieving more than simply collecting a paycheck. It will provide me an opportunity to give back to my local, as well as global, community, while working in a field I am highly interested in. Finally, I believe my prior leadership experience and ability to operate under stress will allow me to thrive.

ANALYSIS

One strength of this essay lies in Zachary's honesty and candor. He informs the reader of all of his internal motivations and expectations and openly admits when he is wrong or misguided. These anecdotes allow the reader to better empathize with and understand him.

The first half of the essay mainly focuses on his experiences as a Marine. This story establishes not only his willingness to participate in high-stakes situations in order to help the sick and wounded, but also his realization of the true impact modern medicine can have on the lives of others. He then pivots his focus in the latter half of the essay to his post-military life. There, he highlights his drive by describing how he worked to translate his newly discovered passion into a potential career. Though he describes several experiences ranging from classes to research projects to fellowships, he fluidly connects them by always relating them to the interests and goals driving him. In doing so, he is able to further emphasize his initiative in pursuing this passion for medicine.

In his concluding paragraphs, Zachary connects his passion for treating infectious disease back to his experiences in Afghanistan. This choice not only gives the essay a sense of continuity but also indicates that he is committed to the original goals that dictated where he is today. In explicitly expressing his goals and hopes for the future, he leaves readers with an understanding of his strong sense of clarity and drive.

—Owen Searle

JACQUELINE BOEHME

Hometown: Winter Springs, Florida, USA
Undergraduate School: Public, University of Central Florida
Major: Molecular Biology and Microbiology
GPA: 4.0
MCAT: 35. PS: 12, V: 11, BS: 12.

ESSAY

A home on fire for the red of my lips; the golden tassel for the sparkle in my eye—who am I, but a mosaic of my experiences? It seems that with every tick of the clock, each breath, and every blink of the eye, a splotch of color is added. Chaos?—Perhaps; the keen eye, however, sees art in the works, a continuous story—a human being.

My own chaos begins in a place of colors and sensations, of ardor and intensity—the Dominican Republic. Between the crowds of warm, bronze skin we boarded and sat in the faded navy-blue cloth seats. The bright sun glinted across the vast Caribbean Sea, and my little island disappeared amidst the never-ending blue. I agreed with the setting. Blue is how I felt. I shut the window, but the sun peeked in, bright and happy. Blue and yellow. That is what I would come to know—dreams and sacrifice all wound up.

Initially, the transition was tough—we were the cool Caribbean colors lost in a sea of pinstriped professionals. I watched my parents struggle through years of low-paying jobs. Despite the pain of sixty-hour weeks, three bright white smiles always fueled the fire—my two brothers and I would be given opportunities my parents never had.

My own passion began its manifestation when a young Hispanic doctor bestowed the gift of free health care to my younger brother, upon suffering third-degree burns; his benevolence left me in awe, admiration, curiosity, and amazement. A rainbow of wonders. Overnight, that red cross of medicine became my dream of helping others, of actualizing their hopes, and of spreading the favor that helped us.

Within a few years, the blackness of fear and near death spilled across our canvas when my father suffered two strokes; nevertheless, the bright sun peeked through his window, and he pushed on. At that point, I more deeply began to realize what it was to have a dream—to endure two strokes and continue as a functional part of society seemed impossible, but proved conquerable to my father, who had a vision for his children. Seeing this, I too aspired.

Encouraged by my parents' ardor and my passion for medicine, I began the execution of my own pursuit. Throughout high school, my desires for the future pushed me to extremes, and developed a side of me that I had never known. As I headed down that path of aspiration, the sun's yellow transitioned into the gold that made up the various state awards I achieved for academic and artistic endeavors. I recall the anxiety at the award ceremony for the first state Latin forum that my high school had ever attended. I felt green—could others see it? Months of preparation had brought me to this moment. My fingernails were still covered in paint. Finally, the judge announced that long yearned for award was indeed mine—First Place in the state.

Life at home, on the contrary, was not quite so glamorous and at the not-quite ripe age of sixteen, I took it upon myself to get my first job, of many to come, at Taco Bell. Four years of high school, thousands of tacos, and hundreds of late nights later, I graduated. Although the blue, yellow, red, pink, and green honors tassels clashed with the royal purple cap and gown, the happiness they brought was far from ignorable—I felt as if the clashing colors evinced the thrashes I surpassed in the process.

To college I brought along the colors of experience that have driven me thus far, and pressed on. My dreams of becoming a doctor matured upon a trip to China and another to the island nations of St. Kitts and Nevis. As a result of both journeys, I hold a new understanding of what it means to be given opportunity. Although I surely never felt unloved or unwanted, throughout my youth I felt unfortunate. Miriam Beard once said that "Certainly, travel is more than the seeing of sights; it is a change that goes on, deep and permanent, in the ideas of living." Never had I truly witnessed poverty, as I did in these countries; on the other hand, never had I discerned happiness under such different circumstances, as in St. Kitts and Nevis, or true respect and inner peace, as in China.

Upon returning from China, the fresh image of a toddler, shoeless and filthy with the dust and grime from the pollution in the air, haunted me. I wanted to make a difference. After much reading, my red cross took on a worldview when Doctors without Borders entered the picture. This time, my red passion mixed with the blue and the yellow of my Caribbean past for a deep purple of desire. Although I had no M.D. yet, I began volunteering at the Shepherd's Hope clinic, inspired by my experiences abroad. This small clinic, founded solely on donations, provides free medical care to those who cannot afford it. As a Spanish to English interpreter working with immigrants, I am constantly reminded of my own background.

At the now ripe age of twenty-one, I have experienced success, pain, happiness, loss, and more. Despite the splashes of unexpected pigment in my life, one thing has always been certain—my dream. I, of blue and yellow origins, will to add a Red Cross of health and altruism to my canvas, and to spread the colors of hope as far as the eye can see. My mosaic of tenacity is continually in the making,

ANALYSIS

Jacqueline commits to a bold style, and it works: throughout, she compares her life to artwork, framing the essay as a collage of colorful experiences. Her evaluation of this collection as "chaos" representative of humanity speaks to a character that appreciates the candidness of human experience and portrays her own experiences as rich and varied. This introduction sets the theme for the remainder of the essay: humanity and diversity.

Jacqueline paints an image of her upbringing, noting with personal emotion the struggle faced by her parents and her family. Importantly, she bears to focus that transformative moment that turned her to medicine, underscoring that it was the "benevolence" of the doctor in saving her brother that awed her to do the same. Her keen and humble observations in these moments as well as in her travels abroad demonstrate her character as holding true compassion for humanity.

This is why it is so powerful when she concludes with a discussion of her efforts to help. Her early volunteering efforts in providing free medical care to the impoverished show a selflessness and a dedication to the mission of medicine; her ability to use her bilingual abilities to bridge the language gap for her patients demonstrates a potential to bring medical care to all. So her dream to "spread the colors of hope" is confident and inspiring.

—George Moe

ANDREW MAUL

Hometown: Portage, Pennsylvania, USA
Undergraduate School: Private, Juniata College
Major: Biology
GPA: 3.93
MCAT: 32. PS: 11, V: 10, BS: 11.

ESSAY

I vividly recall the surge of emotion and chills that ran down my spine as I wandered through the free health clinic in a rural, impoverished Salvadoran town. I met a kind nurse who cared for hundreds of patients by herself. She showed me her two tiny examination rooms, both littered with overly used equipment. It was sobering, but inspiring. No experience has been more impactful than witnessing the need for accessible, quality healthcare, especially in an area so close to my heart.

Twenty-two years ago, my family adopted me from El Salvador. Over that time, they showed me how to care about people, keep a sharp focus on my goals, and always deliver on my word. Their teaching by example, coupled with the realization of just how fortunate I am, has led me to my passion. I want to spend the rest of my life helping others improve theirs, and believe that becoming a physician is how I'll do it.

My decision to pursue medicine began with a great deal of pain. It was the end of my eighth grade basketball season, in the semifinals of a tournament. During the third quarter, I stole the ball from the other team, and dribbled up the court on a fast break. As

I elevated for a layup, an opposing player charged into my body. SNAP! I immediately felt severe discomfort running up my leg, and knew something was very wrong. As the trainers helped me off the court, I watched the swelling around my ankle continue to grow. My first trip to the emergency room resulted in an inconclusive diagnosis, and a scheduled appointment with an orthopedic surgeon.

The next day, I was diagnosed with a fractured ankle, which unfortunately meant my season was over. The orthopedic surgeon's vast knowledge of anatomy and physiology and explanation of my injury using X-rays captivated my attention, and sparked my interest in medicine. Over the next six weeks, I rehabilitated my ankle and returned to sports as healthy and quickly as possible. Grasping the impact of a medical profession, I set out to become a physician.

Setting goals was a habit growing up. Academics and sports were my primary focus, and in grade school, I dreamt of playing a varsity sport and set a goal in fourth grade to graduate as valedictorian of my class. These goals shaped the next eight years of my life, as I learned to balance schoolwork with playing sports. I was determined to excel inside and outside of the classroom, and worked very hard. Throughout high school, I strove for academic and athletic excellence. Through dedication and perseverance, I started for three years in basketball and baseball, was named captain of both teams as a senior, led both teams to playoff appearances, and graduated as class valedictorian.

While my academic and athletic experiences were very fulfilling, the highlight of my time in high school was sharing my love for sports and academics with children. Every summer, I volunteered to help my coaches run camps for kids in kindergarten through eighth grade. During these camps, I taught the fundamentals of the game and emphasized the importance of determination, commitment, and teamwork. Coaching the kids was extremely rewarding, and allowed me to develop an even temper and positive attitude, even in stressful situations. This experience also helped me discover a strong interest in teaching that I hope to develop as a physician.

In college, I've had extensive shadowing experience. One unforgettable moment came in the emergency room when a patient coded. I watched as physicians and nurses urgently tried to stabilize the patient, to no avail. I learned two challenging lessons from the patient's passing: medicine affects patients, their families, and healthcare professionals equally, and witnessing death is unavoidable when working in medicine. These lessons, among many others learned through my shadowing experiences, have provided me with invaluable insight into the daily life of physicians and surgeons, as well as the demands and rewards medicine offers.

Although my shadowing experience was enjoyable, I desired to learn more about the aspect of medicine that shapes clinical practice—research. Through my research experiences, I discovered the intricate relationship between research and clinical medicine. As I spent a summer studying tendon development with some of the world's brightest minds in Boston, the importance of collaboration and perseverance in effectively translating research from bench to bedside became clear. Now, I hope to combine my love for medicine with my research interests to broaden the scope of my work. This approach will be personally fulfilling while enabling me to make a valuable contribution to biomedical science.

Life experiences shape us as individuals. An unfortunate sports injury sparked my interest in medicine, while clinical and research experiences and a visit to a clinic in my birth country further strengthened my ambition. Ultimately, I hope to return to that Salvadoran clinic as a medical student and physician to provide quality healthcare to those in need. I'm excited about moving forward and the opportunities that lie ahead.

ANALYSIS

Andrew begins in medias res, immediately drawing the reader in with his anecdote of the clinic in El Salvador. Through this strong opening, he provides context about where he has come from and how his past experiences have shaped his values, which helps frame the rest of the essay. The essay is ordered chronologically, and he flows from his adoption and childhood to high school to college. In each stage of his life, he shows how different experiences developed his character and passions, making him into the person he is today.

For instance, his ankle injury illustrates how despite hardships and setbacks, he is able to get back up even stronger and continue to excel in what he loves. He also shows that when he is passionate about something, he uses his own internal drive to help others and make the community a better place. This is best exemplified when he outlines his own personal athletic accomplishments but also then describes how he volunteered in sports camps and worked with children in his community.

Overall, Andrew does a great job of illustrating how he has developed different skill sets and passions from his past experiences and how each experience has inspired him to become a doctor. Thus, the reader is able to easily visualize who this student is and how he will fit into the Harvard Medical School environment.

—Melissa Du

JONATHAN FISHER

Hometown: Newton, Massachusetts, USA
Undergraduate School: Private, Yale University
Major: Molecular Biophysics and Biochemistry
GPA: 3.85
MCAT: 34. PS: 11, V: 10, BS: 13.

ESSAY

Jim and I had only spoken once by phone and were now in a soundproof piano practice room in my dorm basement, after dark and out of cell phone range. My new piano student told me he lived in a sober house, was unemployed, and "had time to kill." He wanted to learn piano and called me because he read favorable online reviews of my piano playing. I was somewhat flattered but mostly uneasy about what I was getting myself into.

I have played jazz piano since age 11. My early focus was technique. I loved practicing and spent hours at the piano. Through Boston's Berklee School of Music summer programs, I gained a solid foundation and connected with exceptional musicians. I led multiple ensembles in school and professional circles. At first, I played wherever I could, including non-paying venues, but as my music further matured, I performed at increasingly high-visibility settings. I particularly treasured playing for charitable causes such as Ronald McDonald House, Gift of Life bone marrow drive, and at Boston Children's Hospital. During college, I taught jazz piano, helping my students navigate the complexity and nuance of jazz theory. In the last several years, a highlight of each week was playing solo jazz in Yale's cancer center lobby. Although I could not help patients from the medical perspective, I felt that I made a small contribution when an improvisation on "Somewhere Over the Rainbow" would bring a smile to a patient's face.

To me, there are striking parallels between jazz and medicine. Jazz improvisation encourages freedom of expression and creativity within the confines of a musical structure that is unspoken but understood among performers. Medical practice emphasizes customization of care based on a patient's unique circumstance within the boundaries of established care paths and standards. In jazz, musicians take turns at improvisation, while the rest of the band "comps" (jazz lingo for "accompanies"). A fine soloist leads without overshadowing. Effective comping highlights the soloist without drawing excessive attention. Jazz, dynamic and fluid, requires teamwork and the ability to listen. I believe jazz prepared me well for the seamless teamwork and collaboration, learning, and adaptability that are intrinsic to medicine.

At Yale, I was drawn to Molecular Biophysics and Biochemistry for its scientific rigors and biological applications. A major focus of my work has been laboratory research. Under the guidance of my mentor Dr. Keith Choate, a brilliant physician scientist on the Yale faculty, I identified and studied the function of a palmitoyl-transferase gene responsible for a cutaneous inflammatory disorder called erythrokeratodermia variabilis. I also observed Dr. Choate in the pediatric dermatology clinic at Yale New Haven Hospital. I vividly recall a young girl with brown scaly plaques covering almost her entire arm, her tearful efforts at hiding her arm as if she felt shameful, and her mother wringing her hands in anguish. The medical team approached the girl gently, trying to put her at ease. When Dr. Choate mentioned the potential of genomic-driven medicine offering new therapies, her mother's eyes lit up, even though the solution was not yet at hand. I had been fascinated with the gene from the molecular angle, but seeing firsthand the physical and emotional tolls from the disease strengthened my interest in developing "post-genomic" technologies. At the same time, moments like this remind me why I want to be a doctor. No doubt biomedical research is stimulating and rewarding, and I hope to continue research pursuits. But I want to work directly with patients and personally make a difference in their lives. While it is possible to make a difference through research, I find it particularly meaningful to contribute at the human-to-human level. My aspiration is to learn about the human body and its diseases and impart my knowledge and skills to patients to relieve suffering. Medicine is going through significant changes. There is hope that technologies such as high-resolution genomics may identify more biomarkers for disease diagnosis, prognosis, and therapeutic guidance. Refinements in DNA sequence technology and computational tools already allow higher and higher throughput at lower cost. Application of genetic analytics on a population scale will hopefully help make personalized medicine a reality. Healthcare delivery is also going through a redesign, with increased emphasis on value and teamwork. I look forward to entering medicine at such an exciting time and feel well equipped from my training in molecular biology, computer programming, bioinformatics, and jazz to make a meaningful impact.

After months of piano lessons, Jim played an awesome improvisation of "Mary Had a Little Lamb." We had become friends and shared animated dialogues about art, religion, love, biology, and of course music. Jim was delighted that I also enjoyed rap, his favorite genre. I saw a transformation from aimless addict to proud-yet-fragile young man. And then . . . he got a job! Jim was gainfully employed. He told me I was his inspiration. Little did he know that through the opportunity to teach him, grow with him, and observe his remarkable transition, I was in fact inspired by him.

ANALYSIS

Jonathan's comparison between his two main interests, jazz and medicine, shows how music has given him a unique perspective that makes him stand out from other applicants. From his achievements in music, it is clear that he has developed and honed his leadership skills and his discipline, both of which are extremely applicable to a career in medicine.

Jonathan uses the anecdote in the fourth paragraph to transition into why he wants to pursue a career in medicine, while still incorporating the theme of music. He reveals that despite his enthusiasm for biomedical research, he finds great fulfillment and meaning working with the patients on a more personal level. Thus, he makes it clear to the reader what drives him and why he wants to become a doctor rather than pursuing research or music.

Jonathan frames his essay with an overarching story in which he is greatly inspired by the progress his piano student has made after months of working together. While it may not address any technical skills that pertain to the medical field, this story conveys the main theme of Jonathan's essay: he is passionate about helping others, both inside and outside of the medical field.

—Evelyn Manyatta

LASHYRA "LASH" NOLEN

Hometown: Los Angeles, California, USA
Undergraduate School: Private, Loyola Marymount University
Major: Health and Human Sciences/Public Health
GPA: n/a
MCAT: n/a

ESSAY

My stepfather was a product of a "food desert." Raised in inner-city Los Angeles, his diet was limited to the convenience of fast food. In an environment that fostered unhealthy dietary behaviors he was unable to modify his eating habits and fell victim to a life of morbid obesity. I watched my stepdad lose his mobility with time. When I reached middle school, he could no longer "shoot hoops" with me in the backyard, and instead spent the majority of his day on the couch. Ashamed that he was unable to fit into restaurant booths or comfortably drive a car, my stepfather often stayed at home and eventually became socially isolated. His ability to engage with the world around him became defined by a chronic disease. When I was 16, my stepfather died of a heart attack as a result of Type-2 diabetes. Although I wanted to be a physician since I was a young girl, it wasn't until November 21, 2010, that I realized how imperative it is that I commit my life to advocating for the medically underserved. As an African-American woman in the sciences, I will use my education to ensure that marginalized families are empowered to effectively fight against preventable diseases.

Two years after my stepdad's death, I became the first person in my family to pursue a career in the sciences. Since my first day in college, I have utilized my education to serve marginalized communities. As a freshman, I began volunteering at the Good Shepherd domestic violence shelter (GS); later, as a senior, I was awarded a grant from the Clinton Global Initiative University to create a bilingual nutrition and exercise program for low-income, pre-diabetic women at the shelter. At GS, I was continually inspired by the women's resilience as they worked to rebuild their lives after surviving immense trauma. The strength that I saw in these women reminded me of the strength of my mom, who raised me as a single mother and rebuilt her life after the trauma of losing her husband. Unfortunately, like my mother, the women at the shelter suffered from a host of chronic diseases inflicted by stress. Witnessing the parallels between my own family and the women at the shelter illuminated the extent to which marginalized populations can be excluded from the healthcare system. This discovery further ignited my passion to serve as an advocate for and stand in alliance with the medically underserved.

Witnessing my family and community members navigate an often unfriendly healthcare landscape has highlighted the importance of kinship in medicine. Through my personal and voluntary experiences, I discovered that empathy and kinship are at the core of the patient-practitioner relationship. Kinship is evident in many facets of medicine, from macro-scale patient advocacy to smaller moments, such as the sighs of relief that I heard when Latin-x patients discovered that I speak Spanish. After witnessing the positive impact of speaking a patient's native tongue, I was inspired to further explore methods to improve the healthcare experiences of marginalized communities. As an intern at the Ventura County Medical Center (VCMC), I witnessed homeless patients continuously return to the hospital for the same ailment. I therefore pursued a research project focusing on how a recuperative care facility could help address this problem by providing homeless patients with a safe space to recover from operations. Through diligence and collaboration, the National Health Foundation's Pathway Recuperative Care facility was opened last summer. Notably, my undergraduate experiences highlighted that advocacy is not solely a habit, but a lifestyle. Thus, I have pursued advocacy beyond my undergraduate career, evident through my experiences as a Fulbright Scholar.

My passion for preventive medicine and social justice has amplified during my year as a Fulbright Scholar. At Rafael Puga Ramón High School, I utilize the classroom to lecture on various topics, ranging from food deserts to domestic violence. To supplement my lesson on domestic violence, I am organizing a solidarity march and fundraiser, "Puga Se Mueve," to support an organization that provides resources to domestic violence survivors in La Coruña, Spain. In addition to my advocacy projects, I am conducting research on adolescents' attitudes toward obesity and diabetes to then develop targeted educational materials for teens that promote a healthy lifestyle. My commitment to creating patient-centered preventative health materials and initiatives like Puga Se Mueve has affirmed my desire to become a physician activist.

As I reflect on my work as a Fulbright Scholar, I am reminded of the words of my stepfather, "Shyra, you can do anything you put your mind to"; I have decided to put my mind to serving others. From leading nutrition courses at Good Shepherd Shelter to advocating for homeless patients, I have diligently worked to serve my community. As a physician with an MD/MPH, I will continue to commit myself to studying the upstream determinants of health affecting my patients and vulnerable populations. I strongly believe access to healthcare is a human right and therefore would like to dedicate my studies to serving marginalized patients, like my late stepfather, as a leader in medicine.

ANALYSIS

It is clear from the start that Lash is passionate about preventative care and improving health care for marginalized communities; she establishes this through the story of her stepfather, who suffered from obesity. The main strength of this essay is the clear focus on Lash's aforementioned passion. This focus is maintained throughout the essay and supported by a series of experiences and accomplishments.

First, she mentions her experience volunteering at GS and designing a bilingual nutrition and exercise program. Not only are these activities impressive on their own, but she relates them back to the overarching theme of serving marginalized communities, too. She also discusses her time as an intern for VCMC and as a Fulbright Scholar, providing further examples that highlight her passion for advocacy. Each paragraph serves as an insight to Lash's drive.

In the conclusion, the essay comes full circle with a meaningful quote from Lash's stepfather. She shares her plans as a physician and, one last time, reaffirms her commitment to serving the underserved, which creates a powerful ending to the essay.

—Katharina Wolf

EMILY RENCSOK

Hometown: Detroit, Michigan, USA
Undergraduate School: Private, Johns Hopkins University
Major: Biomedical Engineering
GPA: 3.91
MCAT: 34. PS: 12, V: 11, BS: 11.

ESSAY

Ever since I was in fifth grade, I've wanted to move to Mars. At the end of the school year, my teacher transformed the school courtyard into a "planet," and a third of the class was the astronaut group and the rest were mission control. Though most of the students were excited to watch Apollo 13, I was super stoked to learn about the new planet. Over the course of the night, my mission control team and I supported the astronauts in collecting data that we could then analyze, eventually determining that the new planet was (surprise!) very similar to Earth. Through designing experiments, collecting data, and making discoveries that had never before been made about this planet, this project singlehandedly sparked a huge interest in scientific discovery for me at an early age. I continued to have this passion for discovery throughout middle school and high school, eventually deciding to study biomedical engineering in college after learning about the field when my grandma had her knees replaced.

During my freshman year at Hopkins, I traveled to rural Honduras on a Global Medical Brigade to run a medical clinic for a week. The first patient that I saw was a middle-aged woman who had a parasite infection, fungal infection, and respiratory infection. Learning about the biology of the diseases and medications used to treat them from the doctor was fascinating! At least until the second patient presented with the same conditions. And the third. We prescribed the same medications over and over to treat the same conditions, and I eventually became disengaged from the consultations, realizing that our three-month supply of medications was just a Band-Aid for a much larger problem. Watching patients leave the clinic with more hope and less pain ranks among the most fulfilling moments in my life, but I questioned whether I could spend a lifetime as a medical doctor: the scientist in me was frustrated by just a mere few days of providing surface-level solutions.

Interested in satisfying my planet-exploring, discovery-oriented self but with a newfound passion for medicine, I decided to try a few research projects with an application to medicine to see if I might want to get a PhD. One of my projects, using a 3D bioprinter to make a hydrogel scaffold for use in cartilage repair at Trinity College Dublin, was simultaneously one of the coolest experiences I've ever had but also a complete disaster. On the first day, Dr. Kelly told me that his lab had just purchased the 3D printer and no one knew how to use it, so it was my job to figure it out. In the first month, I broke two needles and the entire printer stopped working because I didn't change the oil. The plumbing clogged so we had to call someone from Switzerland to fix it. Despite having many setbacks like these, I successfully printed scaffolds with mechanical data that could be used in a larger project in the lab by the end of the summer. Seeing my work being used in other projects and eventually submitted to a scientific journal was extremely rewarding, but sitting with that printer for hours every day almost drove me insane. I loved that I discovered something new that could be used in the future, but I often felt very isolated and like the research that I was doing didn't really have a purpose.

It wasn't until I shadowed Dr. Gamper in the pediatric oncology clinic at Hopkins that I finally drew my connection between research and medicine. I had previously done some research in Dr. Gamper's cancer immunotherapy lab but hadn't seen the clinical side of his research. On my first day shadowing, I met an eight-year-old patient who had leukemia and was about to receive a bone marrow transplant. When Dr. Gamper introduced me to him and said that I was a biomedical engineer, the boy said something that I'll never forget: "So can you build tiny robots with two lasers that will kill my cancer cells?" Finally, everything made sense. With that one sentence, I drew the connection between my interest in both research and medicine: I had to do both. The translation from research to patients was there, I just hadn't seen it since I hadn't found something to inspire my research.

I found my passion in medicine in pediatric oncology, and I saw how my passion for research could fit into that. I saw issues every day in clinic that researchers are currently working to solve. I was frustrated that the answer to almost all of my questions for Dr. Gamper was, "It's unclear." I thought about all of the time that I had spent in lab without having this clinical background, and it made my time feel almost useless. Had I found this clinical perspective earlier, my immunotherapy research would have seemed much more relevant, and I would have been better at it since my research would've had a clear purpose. In order to be a successful researcher in pediatric oncology, I realized that not only do I need an MD to understand biologically what is happening with the diseases, but I want an MD to interact closely with the patients and help advance my research to use in clinic.

To answer the patient's question: it might not have two lasers and it might not even be a robot, but I'll find a way to kill those cancer cells, and I'll find a way to actually get it to patients like you.

ANALYSIS

Emily utilizes captivating storytelling to immerse the reader in snippets of her life. Her essay is focused on passion, and it is clear throughout the essay that she is unapologetically herself. This sense of candor is apparent when she admits to being unsure, making mistakes, and being frustrated. It is this authenticity that makes her seem human and relatable and makes her stand out to the reader. In showing how she was able to grow from each situation, she implicitly demonstrates that she is a curious, passionate, and thoughtful problem solver.

Research is a significant part of Emily's life, and she bases the structure of her essay on the different research experiences that she has had that have built upon one another. She artfully communicates how she continually pivoted as she went down her winding path, concluding with a strong claim that relates why she wants to go to medical school: she desires interactions with patients that will strengthen and inspire her research.

—Melissa Du

AGATHA BRZEZINSKI

Hometown: Wilsonville, Oregon, USA
Undergraduate School: Private, University of Portland
Major: Chemistry: Biochemistry and Spanish
GPA: 3.86
MCAT: 33. PS: 12, V: 9, BS: 12.

ESSAY

Standing on the fourteenth tee, I watched my ball bounce gingerly down, down, down, and disappear. On the 288-yard downhill sharp dogleg left I was looking at, I planned to use my trusty draw to land on the green in one shot, putting me in position for an eagle or, at worst, a tap-in birdie. I was in the lead in the district tournament going into this hole, and knew I could do it. I only needed a par, but I had never missed this shot and I thirsted for that eagle. Ten minutes later, however, I watched my third consecutive shot go out of bounds. The crowd went silent. Choking back tears of frustration, I took a deep breath and finally gave in, grabbed a short iron, and played it safe with my very last ball. Although it only took me four shots to finish the hole, I could only stare in disbelief at the ten on my scorecard.

Years later, I learned another lesson in humility as I stood in between a young mother and a nurse in a small urgent care clinic. Despite a passion for foreign languages, I had been terrified to speak to native speakers; deciding not to let my fear control me, I had signed up to interpret Spanish after only having studied the language for a year and a half. "What's wrong?" is a simple enough

phrase to interpret, yet instantly, five different possible transla-
tions had come to mind. I opened my mouth, hoping that something would burst forth from the brain fog, but instead I just stood
there. Looking at the floor while trying to sort out my thoughts as
quickly as possible, I felt their eyes and concerns that maybe I was
not ready for this challenge. Had I overestimated my abilities? Had
I tried for an eagle when I only needed a par?

Despite a rough first day, I kept at it. I volunteered to work with
as many patients as possible, practiced with interpreters during
slow hours, stayed as late as I could, and spoke further with patients
while we waited for physicians. Soon, I found myself learning more
than the Spanish I had come to perfect; as I learned more about
the people who had come to the US from other countries and
heard about the healthcare they had received there, I discovered
an intense interest in international health. I heard life stories and
saw how lack of access to medical care can turn a possibly treat-
able disease into a fatal one, as a young girl was diagnosed with
advanced leukemia. One woman from Mexico, when diagnosed
with diabetes, said she knew it was coming because everyone
in her family had it. When we told her that she could reverse it by
changing her lifestyle, she just stared. "You mean, I don't have to
live with this? I can be cured?" It was my turn to be blown away
at the gaps in medical education, that in a population so highly
affected by this disease, there were people who honestly did not
know that it was preventable.

One dark, rainy January night, it all came together. On my way
out of the door of the clinic, I heard someone yell, "Interpreter,
please!" I returned to find a young woman crumpled over in pain;
she needed to be seen immediately. All at once, everything func-
tioned like clockwork. A nurse took her vital signs while I took
her medical history. One person simultaneously set up a room

while another ran to get the physician. As soon as the nurse was done, I escorted the patient to her room and the physician hurried in. I had never interpreted with such ease and fluidity in my life. The woman complained of pain which, the doctor decided, was due to either a kidney stone or appendicitis, and she was quickly sent to the hospital.

Although I had sincerely enjoyed interpreting, I could not see myself doing it as a career; it lacked the critical thinking and intellectual challenges I loved in my science classes and research. I was sure I wanted to go into medicine, but I was still uncertain of the exact role I wanted to play. Driving home that night however, I was completely elated. Everyone—the physician, the nurse, and the rest of the staff—had worked seamlessly as a team to treat the patient as quickly as possible. Most of all, however, I was impressed by the way the physician specifically had led the medical team, not only with speed, but with true care, concern, and professionalism. Although funds were tight, I had often seen this physician make the most out of difficult circumstances. I had seen him consult with other physicians about difficult cases and had seen other physicians approach him with their questions. To me, he epitomized resourcefulness, compassion, and humility, and I admired him. After that night, there was simply no doubt that the role I wanted to play in medicine was the physician. My experiences volunteering in the ED and in gastroenterology in Poland and shadowing in the ICU further confirmed to me that more than anything, this was the right path for me.

My pride cost me the tournament that day, but the following week for the state tournament, I stood on the same tees, facing the same hole—the same trees, the same water, and the same bunkers, remembering what had transpired the week before. This time though, I knew better. When others pulled out their drivers,

I pulled out my iron. If I am fortunate enough to be accepted to medical school, I know that classes, patients, and rotations will prove tremendous challenges; I fully expect this to be the most difficult thing I have ever done. However, although a long, risky drive may be flashy and impressive, I have learned to manage the courses I play, and in doing so, discovered who I am.

ANALYSIS

Agatha opens her essay with a descriptive anecdote from a district golf tournament she lost. At first, the vivid recounting has no obvious connection to any of Agatha's medical experiences, so she leaves the reader curious to find out how the story will connect to the rest of her essay. However, as she transitions into her next paragraphs, it becomes evident that the themes of humility, persistence, and self-growth present in this introductory anecdote will be central in her path to medicine.

In the body of her essay, Agatha describes her experiences as an interpreter at an urgent care clinic. She takes readers through her feelings of failure and self-doubt and displays a vulnerability that allows them to empathize with her journey of self-discovery. Her descriptions also highlight her introspective nature and her ability to reflect, reason, and learn from her difficult moments in her life.

Agatha concludes the essay by returning to her initial anecdote and reminding readers of how she has grown from the person she was at that golf tournament. In doing so, she effectively relates the sense of resilience and drive she carries as a golfer to how she will approach medical school and her medical career.

—Owen Searle

PERRY CHOI

Hometown: Monterey, California, USA
Undergraduate School: Private, Harvard University
Major: Neurobiology
GPA: 3.9
MCAT: 38. PS: 13, V: 11, BS: 14.

ESSAY

By integrating skills I have gained from conducting translational neuroscience and organic chemistry research, caring for people with Alzheimer's disease (AD), and studying the brain on molecular, cellular, and systems levels, I want to help alleviate one of society's most burdensome and significant issues: mental illness.

My interest in the brain started in high school when I had the opportunity to investigate the neural correlates of music performance with electroencephalography (EEG) in Scott Makeig's computational neuroscience lab at UCSD. An avid musician, I was fascinated by how the brain could represent complex behaviors such as emotional perception of music. This fascination with neural processing eventually pushed me to pursue neurobiology at Harvard.

My freshman year I saw a flier calling for student volunteers to work with people with AD. Interested in neurology, I saw this as a perfect opportunity to learn more about brain pathophysiology. Every week I would go to the nursing home to meet my resident—talking, performing music, or even playing croquet. I learned a lot about caring for people with dementia, experiencing firsthand how simple actions such as communicating with facial expressions and touch, and being flexible in conversations, made a big difference. As I learned these lessons, however, my assigned resident also became my friend. I found myself practicing piano pieces for the first time in years to play for her. Being recognized, a simple action many of us take for granted, became a highlight of my day. When I attended lectures about AD, I no longer visualized patients without faces, but instead saw my friend. She brought personal relevance to my previously abstract academic world, and I began to see medicine as a future vocation.

I wanted to learn more about the interface of academics and medicine and looked for ways to study the mechanisms of the brain in a clinical context. I found such an opportunity in Diego Pizzagalli's translational neuroscience lab at McLean Hospital, where I utilized EEG to study clinical depression. In the process, I gained direct insight on the current state of psychiatric research, the clinical research environment, and how to think critically about unsolved problems. More importantly, by applying my research skills and neurobiology coursework in a clinical context, I experienced firsthand how my passion for academic learning and intellectual curiosity could directly fuel a career in medicine.

In order to better understand clinical practice, I contacted physicians at Salinas Valley Memorial Healthcare System and Massachusetts General Hospital where I shadowed neurologists and cardiologists. I observed regular check-ups, emergency room procedures, surgeries, and the differences between private clinic and hospital environments. The most memorable aspects, however, were the raw vulnerabilities patients revealed. I saw a wife emotionally leave her husband before heart surgery and watched a surgeon complete the procedure. I listened to a distressed couple discuss options for their disabled child because home care was too demanding and met a woman frustrated by her recent aphasia. The thought that I might be able to respond to these vulnerabilities as a practicing physician was powerful.

In my sophomore year, I attended a lecture titled "Resuscitating Psychiatric Drug Discovery" by Dr. Steven Hyman, former Director of the National Institute of Mental Health. Anticipating hearing about exciting developments from the head of psychiatric research at the Broad Institute, I was surprised to hear him instead state that there have been no new mechanisms in psychiatric drug development since the 1950s. Aspiring to enter psychiatry, I was frustrated but thought of ways to train myself to address this pressing need. One of his main points was that drugs bind to brain receptors and interact with catalytic enzymes, yet there is little emphasis placed on the catalysis involved in prescribed drugs. To develop this mechanistic intuition and deepen my understanding of catalytic chemistry, I joined Eric Jacobsen's organic chemistry lab where I have been working to design and discover small-molecule catalyst systems for the ester hydrolysis reaction. Designing, synthesizing, and screening catalysts parallels much of the drug discovery process, and I hope to be able to apply these skills in the future to psychiatric drug development.

I am committed to pursuing a career in medicine. My coursework has prepared me to approach medicine with perspectives from psychology to organic chemistry, and caring for nursing home residents with Alzheimer's disease has given me intimate familiarity with patient care. Shadowing has taught me the physician's perspective, and clinical research has shown me how to mediate collaboration between medicine and academia. In medical school, I look forward to exploring how I can integrate my skill sets to best respond to patient vulnerabilities. Although I am most interested in mental health–related fields, I am eager to explore different fields of medicine and to broaden my knowledge in both the lab and the clinic. By doing so, I hope to learn how to maximize my contribution to medicine and my impact on future patients.

ANALYSIS

The strength of Perry's essay lies in its clarity and structure. Right from the beginning of the essay, Perry makes the reader aware of his primary motivation for attending medical school: his passion for mental health. He then proceeds with a carefully curated chronological set of specific moments and experiences, which each not only shine light on his empathetic, curious, and driven character but also contextualize the evolution of his interest in medicine.

What is remarkably effective about the way he describes each experience is how he reflects on his learnings and then acts upon them. With each transition, his ability to take ownership over his own learning both in and outside the classroom becomes evident, as does his self-aware and impact-oriented nature.

His final concluding statement sums up succinctly his qualifications and the skills and perspectives he can bring from his multitude of experiences. In tying them to his goals for medical school, he finishes off his already strong essay with a clear message: he is both ready and eager for a future in medicine.

—Sabrina Chok

RYAN BARTHOLOMEW

Hometown: Las Vegas, Nevada, USA
Undergraduate School: Private, Duke University
Major: Neuroscience
GPA: 3.93
MCAT: 34. PS: 12, V: 11, BS: 11.

ESSAY

Curiosity about consciousness instigated my interest in the mind from both a philosophical and biological perspective. Particularly inspiring was work by Monti and colleagues, in which they used brain imaging to both identify residual conscious awareness in vegetative patients and establish a means of communication. The complement of medicine and neuroscience alerted physicians to the patients' conscious experience, allowing them the opportunity to better it. While enthusiastic early in college about the promise of studying the mind from the perspective of a physician, becoming confident in my fit for medicine was a gradual process.

My parents, a neonatal nurse and an OB/GYN, initially deterred me from entering medicine. I am grateful for this influence as it has helped make my decision to enter medicine informed. I understand the sacrifices required by the field through witnessing the strain on relationships that can build due to long hours cutting into valuable time with loved ones and by hearing the garage door opening at all hours of the night as my dad rushed to the hospital. The relationships cherished by my dad as he sees patients he once delivered as babies years ago, as well as my mom's pride in the lives of the newborns she saved, are a few of the rewards for these sacrifices.

Making the decision to enter medicine for myself began with analyzing neurological case studies for a neuroanatomy course, when I learned that I enjoy the intellectual challenges physicians face. However, the problems physicians solve belong to people, not to the pages of a textbook. Time spent with hospice patients has provided a better reason to serve as a physician. As a hospice volunteer, all I can offer is a caring presence to people in the twilight of their life; a reminder that they still matter. My first patient's dementia was so severe that I simply sat by his side for many of the visits, a hand on his arm. Yet, sitting in silence provided time to take in the photos and mementos around his room, and appreciate the meaningful life that he had lived, and continued to live. A life that mattered regardless of its condition. The patient himself made sure to not let me forget his continued significance, punctuating weeks of silent visits by suddenly singing along to a nursery rhyme from his childhood that I was playing for him. I enjoy and find fulfillment in both these exciting moments, and the more frequent quiet moments. The eagerness to spend time with these patients, when all I can give is my company, gives me confidence in the appropriateness of my motivation to serve as a physician, when I will be able to give even more.

The passing of friends from hospice highlights the limits of the medicine and procedures a physician can offer. Providing quality care involves being attentive to more than just a patient's physical symptoms, as shown by a nurse while I was shadowing an emergency medicine physician. The doctor triaged the patients, but only the nurse was sensitive to one of the patients' visible signs of guilt and worry. She reassured this patient that the man in the neighboring bed, the man which the patient had injured in a car crash, would be taken good care of. Interacting with people under stress calls for a perceptive approach, as I have learned organizing and leading backpacking trips in Pisgah National Forest for high school students and Duke freshmen. Nervous high schoolers required encouragement, parents concerned about bear safety demanded reassurance, and rain-soaked freshmen needed to see a smile. When visiting hospice patients, there have been times to ask questions, times to talk just for the sake of providing a reprieve from the silence, and times when it was best to embrace the quiet. Most of the people I grew to know through hospice had been robbed of the full use of their mind. Now when I use optogenetics to study the control of behaviors by neural circuits, I look forward to the data not just out of intellectual curiosity, but also because I can see how one day it may help people like those I have met through hospice regain control of their mind and actions. While my passion for research continues to grow with exposure, reinforcing my aspiration for a career in academic medicine, the value I place on patient interaction leads me to pursue an MD instead of the MD/PhD I originally considered. While progress from more limited time spent researching may be more incremental, the quality will benefit from insight gained from greater time spent with the very patients the research is intended to benefit. I want research to supplement my work as a physician, not define it.

Understanding the mind and its conscious experience has significant implications for humanity. Ultimately the goal of medicine is to minimize the painful aspects of this experience and to promote the wellbeing of the body in order to maximize the positive aspects. Progress towards understanding consciousness experience also means progress towards improving it.

ANALYSIS

Ryan discusses the unique value he places on patients' conscious experience of medicine, which he came to appreciate through his undergraduate studies in neuroscience. He uses this frame to exemplify three positive, personal traits.

He begins by demonstrating his *commitment* to the work of a physician by exhibiting his awareness and acceptance of the sacrifices that must be made, through examples such as his parents' round-the-clock working hours. He then illustrates his *"motivation* to serve as a physician" by describing his experience while volunteering at the hospice where he cared for and gave company to patients; in particular, he describes the care he provided to a patient suffering from consciousness impairment. Last, he highlights his *perceptiveness* with his experience as an observant and accommodating leader of backpacking trips during his undergraduate career.

Throughout the essay, Ryan communicates the relevance of his qualities to patient interactions and the work of a physician, indicating that he is not only a promising medical school applicant but also a promising future physician.

—Katharina Wolf

KEIZRA MECKLAI

Hometown: Sacramento, California, USA
Undergraduate School: Private, Duke University
Major: Biology, Minor in Chemistry
GPA: 3.98
MCAT: 524. CP: 130, CARS: 132, BB: 132, PS: 130.

ESSAY

I sat in the US Senate's Hart Building, memo in hand, nervously awaiting my chance to explain the complexities of an FDA draft guidance to staffers working on the Senate counterpart to the 21st Century Cures bill. This FDA draft guidance would, if finalized, increase the regulatory burden on laboratories developing genetic tests. Although nearly all the scientists I interviewed felt this guidance would unreasonably slow the integration of Next Generation Sequencing genetic tests into diagnostics, I learned that their story ignored the many inadequacies which currently plague genetic testing.

As I began to explain my memo, I thought of the first time I watched a doctor offer a genetic test to a patient. Dr. Patel, a geriatric psychiatrist, was offering a test to help determine which drugs might be most effective for her schizophrenic patient. This test seemed to offer an alternative to a frustrating experience that many patients face: trying various medication regimens to see which works best. The patient's excitement was palpable, but I couldn't help but recognize the sad truth that for this patient, a person of color, the diagnostic tools could be less than perfectly reliable. In a world where 80% of the DNA in genetic databases is European, I struggled knowing that these tests are significantly less effective for people of color than for individuals of European descent.

These hidden inequalities in emerging diagnostic tools, when combined with existing inequalities in access to care, have solidified my desire to work as a physician to care for marginalized individuals. As a doctor, I hope to help vulnerable patients access the care they desire while treating them with the respect they deserve, a goal I have looked to advance prior to medical school.

During my first two years at Duke, I had countless conversations with my peers about the pressure they felt to embody "effortless perfection." This expectation, whether self or culturally imposed, created a stigma around speaking out about one's struggles, fears, and insecurities, which in turn led to a wariness towards accessing campus mental health resources. While Vice President of Equity and Outreach on Duke Student Government, I made combating "effortless perfection" my priority. I felt it was time to give students a space to discuss their struggles and make mental health resources more accessible.

These experiences led me to create Duke's first Mental Health Awareness Month. One particular event, a panel for students suffering from mental illness to discuss their experiences, was attended by over 100 students. Through the month's programming, students were able to find strength and support in the recognition that they were not alone in their struggles. As a physician, I hope to leverage this understanding to create a space in my exam room where I work to understand and affirm patients' experiences in the hopes that I can make their illnesses less isolating.

Though it was extraordinarily fulfilling to create awareness of accessible mental health resources, I also sought to combat another impediment to care: access. This year, I have worked to provide abortion access to women who cannot afford their procedures through the DC Abortion Fund. As a case manager, I work with women in all stages of their abortion access process. For some, I simply help them close the gap in their funding. For others, I work with them from start, finding a clinic, all the way to finish, helping to fund the procedure. This work has revealed to me the mountain of circumstances that vulnerable women seeking funding for abortion face. Every time I call a patient, the first question I ask is, "Can I leave a voicemail on this phone and can I identify myself?" This question is a constant reminder that for many of these women, accessing this care is an act of resistance against circumstances outside of their control like homelessness, domestic abuse, and poverty.

One of the patients I aided, Ms. E, found out she was pregnant while at an urgent care appointment for debilitating anxiety. She only learned about the Fund because her physician sat with her in the exam room helping Google resources for abortion care. This physician recognized that without adequate resources, her patient would not have the agency to choose her next steps. As a physician, I will view it as my highest responsibility to understand patients' lives and circumstances. Without understanding the systemic barriers many patients face, I do not believe one can optimally care for a patient. Even when a patient has access to care, I know that treating vulnerable patients demands cultural understanding. While shadowing Dr. Lo, a plastic surgeon in Philadelphia, I saw first-hand how physicians can utilize their knowledge to create a safe space. I watched Dr. Lo work with a transgender-identifying patient seeking cosmetic surgery as a part of her gender confirmation process. Dr. Lo treated this patient with dignity and respect through the simple act of using her correct pronoun, ignoring the fact that her birth name and gender were associated with her insurance. This simple act of recognizing a patient's true identity reminded me of the vital need for good doctors: I can only hope to one day be among their number.

ANALYSIS

Keizra demonstrates clearly a dedication to public service. Throughout the essay, she reiterates themes of responsibility, ethical consideration, and helping the marginalized, which all support that character.

Keizra begins with an introduction featuring her civic participation in the Senate—an eye-catching and impressive experience. The description of her involvement puts forth clearly her values: that progress ought to be paired with ethical consideration. Her presence testifying for policy makers demonstrates an energy to act and understanding of responsibility.

From this introduction, she segues into a backstory that introduces her desire to help marginalized individuals. This admirable theme is reiterated with further concrete examples, including involvement in student government to improve mental health on campus and volunteer service to help provide abortion access to women who could not otherwise afford it. Through these stories, she makes clear that she cares for "systemic factors" that surround treatment. She has taken steps to ensure the safety of patients who may be seeking treatment in adverse contexts and holds an awareness of secondary mental health effects that may surround treatment.

Overall, Keizra's detailed storytelling of numerous relevant and impressive experiences presents a strong testimony of her character and her values.

—George Moe

A.S.

Hometown: Nampa, Idaho, USA
Undergraduate School: Public, Boise State University
Major: Health Sciences
GPA: 4.0
MCAT: 516. CP: 128, CARS: 125, BB: 131, PS: 132.

ESSAY

Behind all action lies a driving force; a love; a passion. That 200×85–foot rink enclosed by hard, wooden boards and transparent plexiglass grabbed ahold of me at a young age. As I laced up my skates, pulled the jersey over my head, and walked down the dark tunnel towards the ice, I visualized myself playing in the NHL; my ultimate dream. I dedicated most of my life to pursuing this ambition, including fifteen years of commitment to training coupled with the sacrifice of living away from my family during and after my high school years to play in the top AAA league in the U.S. At nineteen, I had the opportunity to earn my spot on the top junior team in the U.S., where I would have a chance at being drafted into the NHL. Following the final game of training camp, I stepped off the ice and walked into the locker room. I sat there, soaked in sweat, looking around at the other players. It was silent. The door creaked open and the head coach listed off the names of players he wanted to meet with and mine was first. I briskly changed and took a long walk down the hall towards his office, unsure of what to expect. He expressed that I had great skill, but they needed younger players. Instantly, my hockey career had ended.

Although this unexpected outcome hurt, it allowed me to appreciate how my dedication to hockey, my first true passion, molded me into a strong and capable team leader. I remembered the passionate feelings of playing hockey as I pushed forward in pursuit of a new profession. After pondering the career possibilities a college education could provide, I enrolled in a university and established my new life much different from the routine of practices, training sessions, airports, hotels, games, and meetings. At that time, I sought the feeling of overwhelming purpose and joy that hockey once served. I searched for a challenge that held my interest as deeply as the ice, something I could strive to improve at each day. It was not until I shadowed a sports medicine physician that I rekindled my passion but in a new direction. I became fascinated by the patient interactions and problem-solving required and realized that by pursuing medicine I would need to rely on my focus, hard work, and dedication.

To test the waters of medicine, I worked as a home hospice volunteer where I met my first patient, Brad. We met each week to watch movies together, discuss life stories, and talk about his love for football. Often, he expressed how much spending time together brightened his day. Comments like these, along with his personal requests for me to pray for him, were the moments that emotionally touched and fulfilled me. Over time until his death, I experienced the feeling of improving his quality of life by simply treating him like family. Through our interactions, the void left by the absence of my hockey career became occupied by a new passion: serving others.

I understand the path to becoming a physician requires

extensive sacrifice and commitment. I am excited about the challenge, just as I had been when training as an athlete and entering college as a first-generation student working two jobs to support myself and finance my education. However, I wanted further confirmation that my passion for medicine would pass the test of time before dedicating my future to it. I decided to gain clinical experience as a scribe in the ED. One late Friday evening, the glass sliding doors of the ambulance entrance opened as a young woman was rushed into the trauma bay. She had become asystolic just prior to arrival and appeared to be about my age with a bruised face, spattered with dried blood. The nurse sat on top of her performing chest compressions while the doctor prepared to run the code. Shortly after transferring her to the trauma bed, the physician attempted resuscitation; nothing saved her life. The buzzing of the flat rhythm strip was the only sound present.

Witnessing the physician and EMS staff lose a patient served as a firsthand experience of the emotional challenges associated with medicine. However, through that experience, I realized death may sometimes be an inevitable outcome in medicine, as loss is sometimes an inevitable outcome in life. My desire to pursue medicine grew stronger because this situation reinforced the vast opportunity I will have as a physician to largely impact the lives of my future patients, even though there will be moments when saving a life is out of reach. In those difficult times, my passion for serving others will push me forward.

Medicine is about striving towards betterment, just as I had done with my previous dream. I look forward to the challenges ahead and the rigors of this journey. Through my experiences, I have developed several traits, including dedication, work ethic, and ultimately handling loss, all of which have prepared me to overcome the adversity that lies ahead. And just like hockey, al-

Passion

though each inch forward is accompanied by sheer strength of will and passion, the progress is worth the effort.

ANALYSIS

A.S. describes an impressive successful life-goal pivot that proves to be a testament to their passion and strength of character. They take care to describe the place hockey had in their life so that the unfortunate tryout outcome is clearly established as a catastrophic setback. It is impressive, then, that A.S. was able to make an abrupt turn from athletics to medicine, which they make clear was no small task by describing their pathfinding journey in college.

This journey is recounted fluidly and to a level of personal detail. The logical transition from sports to sports medicine is explained early on and addresses the prime question around A.S.'s circumstance: "Why medicine?" The subsequent patient stories and emergency-room observations grant further detail and depth to their journey and validate their interest in medicine.

Throughout the essay, A.S. takes care in attributing this transformation to character traits of dedication, passion, and strength of will. They recount challenging moments, like witnessing the loss of a patient, and reflect upon these moments as steeling their commitment to helping others through medicine. This delivery affirms their personal values and asserts that their athletic discipline is translatable to medical rigor.

—George Moe

Nina Allen

Hometown: Cali, Colombia
Undergraduate School: Public, University of Pittsburgh
Major: Studio Arts and Natural Sciences
GPA: 3.9
MCAT: 514. CP: 130, CARS: 129, BB: 128, PS: 127.

ESSAY

Monday morning role call in Ms. Penner's first grade class was my recurring nightmare. The explanation of my weekend, always butchered and mispronounced, resulted in constant giggling. I longed for the bell to ring so that I could rush to my after-school art classes where I was more than just the foreign Colombian girl; I was the artist admired by my American peers. Art enabled me to connect to my new home in the United States and eventually led me to establish a sense of belonging in the medical field.

My parents divorced when I was very young. My father was an engineer and travelled extensively. When we did spend time together, we packed in as much exploring of the local museums and exhibits as we could. He inspired my curiosity and instilled in me a desire to understand the natural world. Through my mother, I developed a commitment for making a social impact. We spent many hours together teaching English to other local immigrants in our home communities in Idaho and Texas.

However, the most time I spent as a child was with my Mamita (grandmother). Countless afternoons were spent together, she painting flowers on large canvas, and me covered in paint exploring the use of my body as a paintbrush. Leaving hand and foot prints all over newspapers, I was discovering my own body through art. My art practice has since become the instrument for self-discovery and has helped me discern why I am who I am. It has expanded my curiosity, desire to ask "what if," and ability to problem solve. It has trained my hands and mind to create anything I imagine. It has given me the confidence and liberty to be boldly creative.

At the University of Pittsburgh, I majored in Studio Arts and Natural Sciences. In following my seemingly disparate passions, I had hoped to uncover ways in which the two could be connected. I wanted to dedicate my life to a career in which I could help others, and with my inclination and fascination with science I figured the medical field could be the perfect fit. However, the path between art and medicine seemed uncharted and I first had to discover it.

In my freshman year, I began working in a research lab that encouraged me to forge ahead in doing something so different. In the lab, I used cutting edge technology to create, for the first time, digital sculptures of the face that helped researchers and physicians understand orofacial clefting in relation to facial morphology. It was art. It was science. And it gave me the momentum to pursue a variety of projects ranging from co-authoring a paper comparing facial measurement techniques for surgical procedures to translating medical data from Spanish into English. I later chose an independent research project, which estimated recurrence risk factors of clefting in order to improve genetic counseling for families.

In my lab research, I came to see the ways in which art is integral to medical research. However, I also sought to explore how art could have a more prominent role in the healing process. I applied and was selected for a competitive art therapy internship at the Children's Institute of Pittsburgh. While in this role, I saw how art classes transformed the behavior of students with different mental disabilities. The power of art in healing became more apparent when I volunteered in Colombia at a free clinic for underserved children. At the clinic I saw the opportunity to make the experience of hospitalization less intimidating for young patients. Together the patients and I created handmade games and artwork to make their rooms their own. The act of creating art proved vital to the patient's healing process and I pursued permission and funding to make this initiative an established part of the postoperative care at the clinic. I saw firsthand how art and medicine went hand in hand.

Following my experience in Colombia, I wanted to see how art could be a force of empowerment in my local community. In the fall of 2014, I was awarded a community-based research fellowship to study the transformative power art has on inner city youth at the Manchester Craftsmen's Guild (MCG), an after-school center offering diverse programs in the arts. At MCG I worked in the ceramics room and saw students progressively become more engaged each time they threw a new pot on the wheel. As I have considered art as a tool for empowerment, I wanted to create a link to health, which led me to co-curate an exhibition that brought together undergraduate student artists suffering from mental illness. The goal was to destigmatize discussions surrounding mental illness and to encourage the university to provide art therapy sessions for college students.

I am not exclusively an artist nor exclusively a future physician. I am both. I make art and in being a physician I will also be a healer of health, restoring happiness and well-being. My undergraduate career has uncovered the seamless combination that art has with medicine and it has assured me the possibility to weave the two.

Passion

In a powerful and well-written essay, Nina shares the very unique intersection of art and medicine that she has developed through her undergraduate experiences. She begins with a discussion of where she came from in a way that explains how art became important to her—it was the universal language that connected her as an immigrant to her grade school peers. Nina then tells of her path in turning art into a tool for medicine in order to accomplish her ultimate ambition: to dedicate her life to helping others. In each of the moments she describes along this path, she takes care to explain exactly how she used art to actively improve medicine, which is a very novel and impressive accomplishment.

This essay is particularly effective thanks to its masterful use of language. Nina smoothly transitions between paragraphs in a way that makes the essay cohesive and continuous. She also employs variety in sentence structure and word choice, which keeps the language engaging and interesting. The result is a highly readable and clear testimony that effectively conveys her combined passion for art and medicine.

—Deni Hoxha

Eileen O'Callaghan

Hometown: Seattle, Washington, USA
Undergraduate School: Public, University of Washington
Major: Bioengineering
GPA: 3.87
MCAT: 518. CP: 130, CARS: 129, BB: 130, PS: 129.

ESSAY

Her hand barely spanned the length of my palm, held open to her as she trailed slightly behind me. "We are so close, Hazel, I know you can do this!" I encouraged her. Immediately, Hazel was reinvigorated, and her newfound energy propelled her within my reach. Our hands clasped, and we crossed the finish line together, Hazel, seven years old, beaming with pride, and me, honored to have been by her side. Hazel is one of the many people in my life who has shown me the value of mentorship and been a strong influence in my intense aspiration of practicing medicine.

I had been Hazel's running buddy for ten weeks of training to prepare her for this 5k race through a non-profit program called Girls on the Run (GOTR). As her running buddy, I served as her mentor for questions and reassurance relating to both physical and mental health. GOTR uses creative lesson plans for young girls to instill the value of health with respect to physical fitness, mental development, and healthy relationships with peers. As a strong young woman, I felt accountable to set these young girls on a positive path that would build them to be strong women one day as well. My connection with Hazel, as her mentor and as a resource for guidance in making healthy decisions, is one of the countless motives for me to attend medical school. With my help she accomplished her goal and was on her way to a healthier lifestyle. I believe that medical school will provide me with the ability to educate patients in the pursuit of better health.

With the goal of serving as a resource for others, much of my life has been dedicated to the pursuit of education. While my parents have exhibited continual encouragement, they are unfamiliar with the educational system in the US as they emigrated from Iceland in the mid-1980s. To my parents, the SAT was just the past tense of "sit" with caps lock on. I took it upon myself to reach out to counselors and to those who could help to fulfill my ambitions and bridge the gaps in knowledge my parents weren't able to provide. I deeply respected the relationships I formed and took each piece of advice that I could, becoming a self-motivated student with a strong commitment to community involvement.

My appreciation for those who answered my incessant questions about my future and education inspired me to fill this role for others. I joined the mentorship program in the bioengineering department as a junior at the University of Washington, served on the executive council for my sorority, and worked on several panels in the bioengineering department for prospective students interested in the major. I was thrilled to share my experiences and am confident that I would find further fulfillment if I were able to share wisdom in a significantly more impactful way by gaining knowledge in the field of medicine to offer patients information and opportunity that they might not otherwise be able to access.

Throughout my research, I had the privilege of working closely with a practicing cardiologist. As with medicine, research is rarely an exact science. The cardiologist taught me how doctors should think, always asking more questions so as to engage with the research, just as one should do when searching for a diagnosis with a patient. Confident in my decision to one day be a clinician, I learned from my research mentor the benefit of an engineering perspective, along with clinical experience, in not only answering questions about health, but also in discovering new approaches and solutions to health issues.

Aside from the technical aspects of medicine, a family medicine doctor showed me the importance of the ability to relate effectively to human beings. I recall a patient, a young Arabic woman who spoke little English and who appeared unsure of the white, middle-aged male physician's trustworthiness. The physician was usually affable, extroverted, and confident, but I noticed his demeanor with her shifted; he became calmer and softer. The patient had initially been careful with her words, but after gentle inquiry through a translator, her words poured freely about her chronic stomach pain. When I later mentioned this shift, the physician disclosed that this was very intentional. He emphasized the diversity of patients and how to seek out individual needs based on their language, both spoken and unspoken. Connecting with his patient, despite their vast differences, with the intent of working together to improve her condition, strongly resonated with me.

With each shadowing experience, I have learned more how to recognize differences and adapt to get along with, and feel compassion for, people with any background. A similarity I know will never change between patients and myself, as a future physician, is the aim for optimal wellbeing. I hope to provide my patients with the attentiveness they deserve and in the manner they need to express themselves to offer the best care for each individual. For me, going into medicine is a way to pay forward compassion and dedication I have been shown. I look forward to being a physician so that I can reach my hand out to patients, just as I did with Hazel,

Passion

and pass on as much knowledge and care as possible, to bring them closer to crossing the finish line of good health.

ANALYSIS

The success of this essay lies in Eileen's central focus on one key passion—her commitment to connecting with patients—and her ability to weave together multiple experiences and stories that work together to demonstrate this quality.

Eileen begins with a moving story from volunteering at Girls on the Run, poising it as a demonstration of the level of investment she has placed in a nurturing relationship. Her note on the struggle she faced in navigating the American education system as a first-generation immigrant shows even further a unique drive and discipline. These formative experiences stand as a strong supporting backdrop to her later research and shadowing experiences, communicating that her personal commitment in past activities will carry forward to the pursuit of medicine and quality care as a physician.

Eileen drives home this point in the final two paragraphs as she discusses the importance of compassion and connecting with patients; her own observation of her mentor's techniques demonstrates her attentiveness and care in this regard and speaks to a strong potential to learn from and contribute to the medical community.

—George Moe and Rebecca Lisk

JOHNATHAN WESLOW

Hometown: Richardson, Texas, USA
Undergraduate School: Private, Washington University
Major: Biomedical Engineering
GPA: 3.9
MCAT: 38. PS: 13, V: 11, BS: 14.

ESSAY

As Dr. Hotchner ruffled his patient's sheets, I was horrified by what he unveiled. The face underneath was mauled, and through its swelling I could barely identify a boy only slightly older than myself. "He was pushed out of a moving car," Dr. Hotchner told me. In a matter of moments, this boy had been reduced to a state so weak that an infection could throw him into a whole-body inflammatory state called sepsis, threatening to kill him. It was then that I understood the motivation behind Dr. Hotchner's sepsis research and I received my first introduction to academic medicine. My teaching, clinical shadowing, and research experiences have only fortified my desire to follow in Dr. Hotchner's footsteps. As an academic physician, I would be able to confer my knowledge to the next generation of physicians while also translating research from the bench to the benefit of my patients.

Throughout my undergraduate career, teaching has been my way of relating my experience and knowledge to people of all different ages and backgrounds. The diverse accomplishments that resulted allow me to understand what I would gain from teaching as a physician. My students gave me a true passion for what I was teaching. As the first Math/Engineering Chair of the Texas Academy of Math and Science (TAMS) Research Organization, I shared my appreciation for research with my peers by helping the next generation of TAMS students find research opportunities. I applied my high-school competitive swimming skills as a water safety instructor at my local recreational center. As a computer science teaching assistant in college, I helped many of my peers to build a mode of thought with which I watched them transform their daunting computational visions into reality. The strife and triumph I shared with my students reminded me of the value of my knowledge and the difference that I can make in others' lives as long as I retain faith in its power.

When I shadowed Dr. Nastaran Abadan, a family practice physician, I was delighted to discover a similar role in the clinic. One somber-looking patient came to the office with a severe cold. As Dr. Abadan was explaining the patient's condition, the patient began crying in frustration that she had been consistently sick for the past several months. Dr. Abadan immediately empathized with her and reassured her that by making some small changes in her exercise routine, diet, and supplements, she could build a stronger immune system and ultimately a healthier lifestyle. When the patient's condition improved and she revisited, I could relate her look of triumph and the thrill I felt for her sudden progress to many similar instances I had experienced teaching. Dr. Abadan's unwavering faith that her advice could make a difference, even against something as commonplace as a weak immune system, amazed me. As an academic physician, my faith in the impact that my advice can have will be two-pronged: it will empower me to pass down my appreciation for medicine to budding physicians and allow me to exert a lasting impact on my patients.

My research experiences have provided another opportunity for me to apply what I learned in my curricular life. In high school, my captivation with math led me to apply to TAMS, where I received a research scholarship to statistically analyze the clinical effects of Hyzaar, a pharmaceutical, on subject blood-pressure profiles. After I learned the power that math has to explain medicine, my captivation with math was transformed into a fascination for applying math to medicine. I was motivated to study biomedical engineering at Washington University, where I learned the skills necessary to solve a medical problem from an intrinsic mathematical perspective. After teaching computer programming for two years, I wondered how computer science, similarly to math, helps to probe the barriers of medical knowledge. In an independent study under Dr. Kurt Orbis, I studied how LWPR, an algorithm for nonlinear function approximation, could serve as a potential model for motor memory formation. My astonishment with how easily these programming skills bridged to the medical field compelled me to see how my other classes were related, and this August I will explore how biomedical engineering helps to reduce global barriers of care in a rural Chinese orthotics clinic. Through scientific projects, I learned to apply my curricular knowledge for another purpose: to build a stronger foundation for clinical practice.

My passion has been for applying the wisdom I gain in my curricular life by applying math to medical research and relating knowledge to a diverse set of people. In medical school, I hope to learn to enhance the linkage between math, medical research, and clinical practice. I hope that I can develop from a skilled teacher into an inspiring physician. As an academic physician, I ultimately hope to linger on the intersection of researcher, teacher, and physician: bringing research to the forefront of medicine and the needs of medicine to the forefront of research, inspiring budding physicians as so many physicians have inspired me, and ensuring that

Passion

the benefits of both medicine and research reach peoples of diverse ages, backgrounds, and cultures.

ANALYSIS

Johnathan centralizes his essay around his passion to become an academic physician and builds upon this theme throughout his essay with a mixture of anecdotes and self-reflection. He begins with a vivid recounting of his introduction to academic medicine. Its strength lies in its brevity; though short, the anecdote provides sufficient context for readers to understand the significance of the event and hooks them into learning more about his story.

His next couple of paragraphs elegantly weave together distinct experiences that have shaped his relationship with education and medicine. The essay structure is well organized, with a clear arc in the narrative. Each paragraph conveys important insights into experiences that have encouraged Johnathan to continue to pursue academic medicine while showcasing his diverse interests, accomplishments, and active extracurricular involvement. His conclusion provides a powerful declaration of his aspirations—in drawing from aforementioned experiences and outlining specific goals, he leaves readers with a clear sense of his genuine passion for the field.

—Sabrina Chok

II. INFLUENTIAL FIGURE

DEREK SOLED

Hometown: Randolph, New Jersey, USA
Undergraduate School: Private, Yale University
Major: Sociology and Biology
GPA: 3.95
MCAT: 513. CP: 127, CARS: 128, BB: 129, PS: 129.

ESSAY

If my DNA could be extracted from an inanimate object, that object would be my grandpa's address book. It represents his and my determination to connect with those around us and have a life devoted to service.

I remember that worn leather address book jostling next to the oxygen tank in the pocket of my grandpa's wheelchair as I pushed him up the intimidatingly steep hill located near the exit of the zoo. "I'm going to win. I'm going to win . . . I'm going to beat this thing," my grandpa hollered, laughing.

He didn't win—not in the traditional sense. Two years later, when I was nine, he died of a rare lung disease, although he lived far longer than his doctors had predicted.

Only after his death did I open his address book. It was filled with the names of hundreds of people who had dined in his home. Despite rising to become a prominent dentist, my grandpa, whose immigrant parents died when he was twelve, never forgot his roots. Virtually every Friday night he brought home patients and friends who lacked family and were oftentimes financially unstable. Aside from his sincere kindness, he wanted to make sure that his daughters saw that even in their comfortable town, not everyone was so fortunate.

My parents, too, both university professors, wanted to expose me to the world's realities. As in my grandpa's home, there were always extra places set at our dinner table on Friday nights. Moreover, beginning when I was in early elementary school, my family has traveled twice a year to underdeveloped nations or economically disadvantaged regions of the U.S. My parents wanted my sisters and me to experience life outside our comfort zone, and we often stayed and interacted with people in areas that were far from traditional tourist destinations.

In Tunisia, I walked down streets lined with churches, mosques, and synagogues existing peacefully side by side while religious-based violence erupted not far away. In Senegal, I helped a mother watch her nine children and could see the love that she had for each one, although they together constituted part of what others view as an overpopulation problem. In Haiti, I played soccer with boys who lived in mud shacks with tin roofs and no electricity; but they took pride in the sport, and you would never imagine their living conditions if you saw their field. In New Orleans, I helped build small houses for the homeless after Hurricane Katrina and listened to the future residents of those houses play musical gigs at local soup kitchens because they considered themselves blessed.

Largely due to these experiences, I've always wanted to get close—close to the people and the real problems. After my freshman year of college, I participated in a study abroad program in China on population aging. I learned that China, adopting a Western idea, had increased its number of nursing homes to house its growing elderly population. For my research project, I visited nursing homes to analyze how the people were adapting to this new trend. I didn't specifically go to study medical outcomes, but

Influential Figure

I quickly discovered that many nursing home residents had high blood pressure and frequent colds. I then checked on the health outcomes of elderly persons who instead lived with their children, i.e., those whose families had adopted the traditional Chinese emphasis on filial piety and care for one's parents. This latter group appeared to fare much better than their nursing home counterparts, leading me to conclude that there are certain tangible medical benefits in allowing people to grow older and stay in communities near family and friends.

A year after this trip, I was in my biochemistry lab researching the dynamics of certain amino acids and corresponding effects on whole proteins when I had a "eureka" moment. Waiting for an experiment to conclude, I read "The Social Organism," an essay in which sociologist Herbert Spencer envisions society itself as a living organism. I began thinking about sociology as a discipline that examines many of the same questions as biology, namely how individual parts interact with the whole and vice versa, but from a different perspective.

I became fascinated by the interconnectedness of the natural and social sciences and how their intersection shapes health and treatment of disease. Medically, I realized that although biology is, relatively speaking, the same everywhere, health is a political issue insofar as it is culturally defined and valued. And, I recognized that medical outcomes and experiences are always influenced by social elements. For these reasons, I believe the immersion in and study of other societies and cultures is fundamental to improving health care.

Ultimately, I want to be a physician as well as a leader in health care policy. In addition to nurturing the well-being of my patients, I want to tackle what I consider to be the greatest challenge in medicine in the 21st century—rampant disparities in health care—which, in my mind, can best be addressed by having a multidimensional understanding of the people being served.

I plan to construct an address book of my own like my grandpa's, which still rests on my desk. I want to help a new generation of people reach the summits they seek with their own grandchildren.

ANALYSIS

An important strength in Derek's essay lies in the strong theme that unites each and every paragraph within the personal statement. From the onset, Derek makes clear that fundamental to his character is his determination to connect with and to serve others. He utilizes this central theme to guide us through the lessons and values his upbringing and travels instilled in him and the moments that first drew him to medicine. In doing so, he makes readers aware not only that he has reflected deeply on his desire to pursue a career as a physician but also that he holds both the empathy and passion necessary to do so.

In the latter half of his essay, Derek elegantly connects different key experiences like his research project in China and his realizations within a biochemistry lab to describe how they have inspired his interdisciplinary approach to medicine. He maintains a clear thesis: to improve health care for individuals, we must understand those we are trying to serve. This is a fitting transition as he declares his aspirations to become both a physician and a policy maker. In tying these thoughts, he effectively demonstrates his commitment to being a compassionate and understanding doctor.

—Sabrina Chok

LOGAN CARTER

Hometown: Darien, Connecticut, USA
Undergraduate School: Private, Bates College
Major: Neuroscience (Major), Mandarin (Minor)
GPA: 3.89
MCAT: 31. PS: 11, V: 9, BS: 11.

ESSAY

I yearn for a profession that weaves human connection, challenge and innovation into my everyday life. Each morning, like millions of others, I stand in front of the sink, toothbrush in hand, and reflect on the image of my half-conscious self in the mirror. I am blessed with an able body, a sound mind, a voice and a supportive family. I am incredibly grateful, and through medicine I will work arduously to enlighten others with the optimism to thrive and the gift of a healthy life. I have never felt more eager to commit myself to this process.

Life thus far has guided me on a dynamic journey. As a son, I have lived the jarring roller coaster that accompanies a parent's diagnosis with cancer. As a camp founder, I have seen the eyes of a child who cannot wait to show you his latest creation. As an EMT, I have listened to others in the heat of car accidents, miscarriages, three a.m. falls and screaming children. Through it all, I have maintained a positive outlook and learned the true power of honesty, patience and mutual respect.

I remember standing in the kitchen before just another day of high school when my dad told me there was a tumor the size of a tennis ball pushing up against his brain. I was fifteen years old. At the time, the word tumor did not register as synonymous with cancer, and yet it soon became apparent that things were going to change. My family, mom and dad, two brothers, a little sister and a dog, moved that summer. I started in a new school, began studying to become an EMT, and over the next two years, saw hundreds of patients. Young, old, rich, homeless, scared, angry, dejected, some were fighting for their lives, and some were in sheer agony. Yet with each call, I met a new face. I grew fonder of opportunities to hear patients' stories, talk with their families, and connect through the most basic forms of human communication.

Meanwhile, my dad grew sicker and sicker. Amidst splitting headaches, he forgot our birthdays and names, before losing his ability to form sentences. I spent the last two weeks of his life shadowing surgeons at Stamford Hospital, and walked to hospice every evening to sit and reflect. My externship ended on a Friday, and I vividly recall the labored breaths I noticed while with him that afternoon. He passed away a few hours later, on my parents' anniversary, my mom and I by his side. I remember a strange feeling of relief amidst the uncontrollable sadness; I knew he was no longer suffering.

After my dad's death, I embarked on a quest to find a new sense of rhythm. Inspired by his disease, I fell in love with the puzzles of neuroscience. I was elected as captain of the sailing team, conducted interviews for the admissions office, and built relationships with friends that will last a lifetime. I lived in Beijing, China, where I absorbed a new and vastly different language and culture, and I combined functional MRI with the ancient practice of acupuncture to closely analyze the brain. I explored healthcare investments through pharmaceutical trials and in my current job, I work every day to find new ways to improve critical care.

Influential Figure

In my time at Brigham and Women's Hospital, I have come to appreciate how medical professionals tirelessly collaborate to better understand organ systems, disease, pharmacology, healthcare access, and the impact of quality patient care. In addition to discussions about facial reconstruction and "death with dignity," I experience the daily routine of clinical research and understand the vital role it plays in advancing medical standards. These encounters undoubtedly incite my already insatiable curiosity to push the boundaries of healthcare and medicine. I am left in awe at the breadth of undiscovered knowledge.

My fervent belief in the power of personal connection separates me as a candidate. Coupled with my intense dedication to others, and my strong desire to think outside the box, I strive to be an exceptional doctor: a caring teacher, mentor, leader and innovator. I strive to maintain a calm presence and never settle for mediocrity. I strive to use every mistake as a learning opportunity. And I strive to connect. I am honest, hard-working and committed. I communicate effectively, I am open-minded to criticism, and I am calculated in my decision-making. I am empathetic, passionate and resilient.

I acknowledge that, like everyone else, I am simply human. I know that medicine is not an easy road, and I expect for it to knock me down. But in seventy years when I catch my reflection in the mirror, toothbrush in hand, I want to see someone who lived with determination and empowered others to overcome adversity. It is at this time that I will be humbled, knowing that I dedicated my life to helping others become physically, emotionally and spiritually complete.

ANALYSIS

One strength of this essay is Logan's ability to weave together many of his life experiences in a cohesive and candid way. Through vivid descriptions of the most impactful moments of his life, he writes an evocative narrative that allows readers to empathize and to connect with him on an emotional level.

The body of the essay seamlessly alternates between Logan's struggle with his father's sickness and his experiences in medicine both as an EMT and as a hospital intern. As he takes readers through each progression of his father's disease, he gives them insight into how he found solace in medicine during this difficult time of his life. It becomes clear that his father's battle with cancer has instilled a passion for medicine in him and will continue to drive and motivate him.

In his last paragraphs, Logan concludes with a strong declaration of his character and values. He is forward with his strengths, clearly outlining what he believes sets him apart. His repeated use of the phrase "I strive . . ." is particularly effective; he builds rhythm and momentum into his words while emphasizing his constant pursuit for growth and improvement. Logan ends the essay as it started, with him standing in front of the bathroom mirror and reflecting on his dedication to his goals. By using the same imagery, he reminds readers that he wants to dedicate his life to this endeavor and leaves them with the impression that he is a reflective and determined individual.

—Owen Searle

HAZEL W.

Hometown: Jacksonville, North Carolina, USA
Undergraduate School: Private, Harvard College
Major: Bioengineering
GPA: 3.8
MCAT: 521. CP: 131, CARS: 131, BB: 130, PS: 129.

ESSAY

There are not many situations in which the ability to read could make the difference between life and death. I witnessed one such situation while shadowing Dr. Imani Williams, a cardiologist in my hometown. While Dr. Williams talked with an elderly patient to update his prescription list, we discovered that the patient was illiterate. Though not a complete shock in itself, it was alarming to come to that realization while rummaging through an entire gallon bag's worth of identical orange pill bottles that contained medications that were crucial for managing his conditions. Fortunately, the patient's wife sorted his daily medications, but the appointment revealed that she had understandably confused several aspects of her partner's complicated prescription regimen. I began my time at the clinic anticipating that my interest in medicine would be further invigorated by learning about details of how various cardiovascular diseases are presented in patients, but this moment and others like it had a far greater impact on me.

No amount of medical textbook expertise would have helped Dr. Williams give that patient and his wife the explanation they needed. My early impression of a physician's work revolved around two ideas: a physician continuously learns about the human body and then works long hours to apply that knowledge to solving patients' issues. I developed this understanding as I grew up seeing my father, a physician, doing both. What I did not fully realize was that medicine was full of scenes like the one I witnessed that day, in which the science was put aside, and a physician takes on the role of an educator instead of a learner. Over time, I have come to understand medicine as much more than an investigation into the human body—it is the ultimate means of equipping others with the information necessary for them to take control of their health, arguably the most important aspect of one's life. I am drawn to the medical field because I feel motivated to be an instrument of empowerment for others, and I see medicine as a compelling way to do that.

This motivation originates from an appreciation of how much I have gained from sources of empowerment throughout my life. From parents who could afford to purchase any book I needed, to several teachers who always encouraged me to push further rather than be content, I have been the fortunate beneficiary of tangible resources and wise insights that put me in a position to thrive. As my recognition of this privilege has grown, so too has my desire to be a similar resource to others. One way this desire has been manifested is in my efforts as a teacher and mentor for underprivileged young students. It has been incredibly fulfilling to be a positive presence in the life of students who need it, whether through providing help with homework, offering insight into the college admissions process, or simply being a positive role model. I hope to also realize my desire to enable others to ultimately achieve more in life as a physician.

In addition, the experiences I have had working with students in afterschool programs mirror many of the aspects of medicine that appeal to me. I began to realize the parallels while volunteering at a free medical clinic for uninsured and financially-disadvantaged patients in my hometown area. In the same way that I approach each child I work with as more than a brain in need of knowledge, each patient at the clinic was approached as far more than a disembodied version of their ailments. Instead, every part of the patient's living experience was weighed by all the healthcare team as medical care decisions were made, like how a changing work schedule might impact a patient's ability to make appointments, or where the most convenient pharmacies and diagnostic centers are for a patient with no car. Just as developing an understanding of my students' and mentees' backgrounds allows me to tailor my lesson plans and advice to their specific needs, I saw how the clinic's physicians took the time to understand their patients' lifestyles rather than simply prescribe medications that temporarily mask an ongoing issue. Doing these things requires more effort, but in the long run, I appreciate how this is truly effective treatment for the patient and I would enjoy doing the same as a physician.

As I continue my pursuit of medical school, I recognize the importance of both the scientific knowledge I would receive and the human skills I would gain there. The necessity of having a firm academic understanding of medicine and the human body is not lost on me as someone interested in doing research at the intersection of medicine and tissue engineering. However, for every patient who might receive the treatment they need as the result of a physician's knowledge of a specific medical fact, countless others only need a person to take the time to understand their situation and offer insight to empower them to better handle their health issue. The opportunity to provide that insight for patients as a physician makes medicine an incredibly alluring career to me.

ANALYSIS

In an illustrative introduction, Hazel describes how they came to care for the *human* dimension of medicine, that "textbook expertise" is not enough to provide adequate treatment to many of the patients who need it most.

Potently, Hazel reflects upon how this insight was transformational to them, having come from a situation of relative privilege; by detailing how circumstances can affect the human dimension of treatment, they demonstrate their ability to consider these issues and that these issues truly matter to them.

The essay aptly rounds off this reflection with an assertion of purpose: to help patients "understand their situation and offer insight to empower them to better handle their health issue." This conclusion draws upon the support built by the details from the introduction and the body of the essay to affirm Hazel's commitment to this human aspect of medicine that they wish to forward.

—George Moe

BRIAN YANG

Hometown: Ann Arbor, Michigan, USA
Undergraduate School: Private, Harvard University
Major: Neurobiology
GPA: 3.99
MCAT: 37. PS: 14, V: 11, BS: 12.

ESSAY

"River rat pride!" I looked up from the metallic charms in my hand
as these familiar words rang through the monotonous buzz of the
Ann Arbor Art Fair crowd. In front of me stood an old friend,
with arms extended, ready for the inevitable embrace ahead. It
had been more than a year since Kevin and I played our last high
school football game together. Returning to my hometown for
the summer after my first year of college, I had expected to bump
into longtime companions and reminisce about days gone by, but
I could not have anticipated how our next conversation would propel me towards a career in medicine.

   Admittedly, my upbringing did not portend that of a future
physician. I grew up in a family full of engineers. Gears and circuits filled my childhood, where I learned about the nuances of
repairing a manual car window before my first trip to the emergency room. College was no different. A boundless road map of
possibilities lay ahead of me, and I was committed to exhausting
each option. Before long, the brain, with its boundless abilities and
unsolved mysteries, became my passion. As an avid breakdancer,
I struggled to comprehend how a single organ could accomplish

so much, synthesizing my movements with the music around me while allowing me to release my emotions and anxieties. It housed my memories, my personality, my identity. The wonders of the brain fascinated me, but I did not fully appreciate its blessings until my reunion with Kevin.

Talking with Kevin that afternoon, I was expecting stories of new experiences and inspirations as he pursued his goal of becoming a teacher. Instead, multiple undiagnosed concussions had left him debilitated, a shell of the savvy, dependable teammate from my memories. He had trouble holding a job, often forgetting what he was doing or when his shifts started. Bright lights or loud noises made him nauseous. Even focusing on reading a news article was a struggle for control. "But hey," he said, "at least now I get all the time I want on my exams." I managed to crack a weak smile as flashbacks of hitting drills and manic coaches raced through my mind. A feeling of helplessness washed over my body as I searched for any actions, words, or gestures to help—but nothing surfaced. I wanted to help. I needed to help, but what could I do? My desire for care had been established, but the skills I needed had not yet materialized.

Searching for ways I could make an impact, I joined the Sports Legacy Institute Community Educators to increase awareness, education, and diagnosis of concussions by guest speaking at local school presentations. As a former football player, my first-hand experiences with the devastation of undiagnosed concussions provided a real-world lens for the student-athletes to connect with. The possibility that our presentations could prevent even one student-athlete from experiencing Kevin's hardship filled me with a humbling gratification, driving me to share with more students, while still appreciating the substantial impact that helping a single individual could have. Working to prevent others from experiencing what Kevin had to endure filled a void, but I still yearned for more.

I found what I was searching for after shadowing Dr. Johnson, a neurosurgeon at my local hospital. What started off as a regularly scheduled aneurysm clipping soon escalated when she was called to perform an urgent tumor removal. Her composure in the face of adversity was both inspiring and humbling. Meeting with the patient's family, I could not help but sense an air of vulnerability fill the room. The loss of control crept its way onto the faces of the family in front of me. The look was all too familiar, recounting the same emotions I felt in my conversation with Kevin. This time, however, the outcome was different. I witnessed how a few well-chosen words calmed the anxieties of twin sisters who entrusted Dr. Johnson with the well-being of their father, how her sage demeanor gave a mother the strength to stand stout for her worried daughters. I beheld the effects on friends and family when a loved one's passions are wrestled out by injury or illness and saw how much autonomy a patient loses when he or she enters the hospital, searching for a sense of control once owned. Dr. Johnson's ability to return a sense of that independence struck me. It became a goal I would strive to attain through a career in medicine.

These experiences have fostered an admiration of medicine that I could not have imagined. I saw firsthand the powerful difference a doctor can make. A career in medicine goes well beyond an interest in science, but is driven by an interest in people and a desire to serve those in need. Patients lose a feeling of independence once they enter the hospital, entrusting their well-being to the physicians that oversee their care. I hope to one day enter a patient room and return some autonomy to my patients. No longer do I wish to feel frustration and helplessness when someone is in need. Medicine offers an opportunity for me to pledge my knowledge, compassion, and desire towards alleviating the burden, for the patients and their loved ones.

ANALYSIS

The strength of this essay lies in Brian's ability to effectively showcase his commitment to and excitement for a medical career by weaving together two separate experiences, while also highlighting his ever-growing interest in the medical field. He begins with the first experience: his reunion with his friend Kevin. This moment helped spark his interest in medicine and led him to seek opportunities to impact the lives of others through the Sports Legacy Institute Community Educators, which helps to highlight some of his accomplishments. His experiences give insight into his ambition and fervor, making him an attractive applicant.

Brian provides a clean transition in the essay by connecting this encounter with Kevin to the second experience he had as a neurosurgeon's shadow. He expresses his admiration for how Dr. Johnson was able to exude a calm demeanor and alleviate stress when interacting with the patients, something Brian was unable to do in his initial interaction with his friend. He connects this to his overarching goal of serving others and improving the patient experience, demonstrating his passion for medicine.

—Katharina Wolf

GREGORY HAMAN

Hometown: Cary, Illinois, USA
Undergraduate School: Private, Carleton College
Major: Biology and Philosophy
GPA: 3.67
MCAT: 37. PS: 14, V: 12, BS: 11.

ESSAY

As Deo stopped talking and drifted out of consciousness, his head sagged and his body went limp. Suddenly his limbs struck out violently, struggling. His muscles locked as his back arched. Finally, he collapsed. Shortly thereafter he regained consciousness, sat up and began conversing as usual. Called from my home in rural Tanzania by a gang of excited students, I had trekked with them through the darkness of night as we carried Deo, unconscious, to the witch doctor's home. Having arrived, I sat in helpless agony watching Deo's cyclic fits. I weakly asked, "Has he taken any medication?" "We don't run to the needle," his parents replied, a bit of Swahili folk wisdom meaning that only if the witch doctor failed would they consider alternatives.

I did not dare suggest that Deo's condition was not caused by, as all others present seemed to believe, "bad spirits." Nor did I criticize the treatments that I witnessed: covering Deo in cloth as he breathed the fumes of burning brush until passing out, drinking concoctions made from various powders and cutting his chest with a razor blade and rubbing liquids into the wounds. Having already witnessed several fits which were occurring at hourly intervals and frustrated with the situation, I offered to pay for a van to carry Deo to a distant hospital so that he might be seen by a medical doctor. After all, I suggested, if that treatment didn't help he could always return to the witch doctor. With neither medical knowledge nor access to it, I had nothing more to contribute.

I already knew that Deo had a history of medical problems. Complaining of joint pain too great to bear, his attendance in my classes was poor. A terrible sort of acne scarred his face, ever unable to heal before new eruptions developed. Was this somehow connected to his convulsions? Despite his condition, Deo's spirit was indomitable, having already soared to the peak of Mount Kilimanjaro with me on a field trip. As President of our Debate Club, Deo led his peers with an unfailing determination to improve their English and had been instrumental in building our club up from one debate each semester to several debates each week.

After offering what assistance I could to Deo and his family, I left the witch doctor's home and returned to my secondary school, focusing on my work as a teacher in the Peace Corps. In the "bush" school where seven teachers and I struggled to offer an education to 500 high school age students, we found ourselves in a system deprived of resources. Most importantly, our school needed more teachers. Although I could not bring them, I promised my students that I would teach them after school, on the weekends and during vacations free of charge if they would attend. The first time we met after school, I looked into seventy upturned faces and saw hope.

If my students were drinking gourds, then I was filling them with knowledge. Day after day, drip after drop, we worked relentlessly, increasing the odds that they would experience a fuller life. Drip! Kened Ndomba can distinguish adjectives from adverbs in the English language. Drop! Sairis Nombo knows more about babies and base pairs than she ever would have. Perhaps most importantly, in a village as threatened by AIDS as ours is, they both know and will never forget their ABCs (Abstain, Be faithful, use a Condom).

Three days after carrying Deo to the witch doctor, his parents called me from outside of the classroom in the middle of a lesson. His condition had not improved so we made the journey to a distant hospital as he continued to have episodes on the floor of the van. Upon arrival, Deo was given Dilantin and quickly settled down. Passing the night without incident, he returned home the following day, pills in hand, and suffered only a single episode the next week.

After three years as a part of Deo's community, I understand the unique sacrifices necessary to work with the underserved. I also know the unparalleled satisfaction of teaching Kened and Sairis lessons that they otherwise would not have been taught. It is the voices of those living without access to basic services that call me to a career in medicine as a doctor who cares for the underserved.

I have witnessed how poverty, unemployment, homelessness, a lack of transportation, and barriers to communication limit access to healthcare in both Tanzania and the United States. A critical facet of my medical school education will involve learning how we can overcome such complex challenges in order to ensure quality care for all patients.

As a physician, I envision myself as a community catalyst, consensus builder, founding member, tireless advocate, project coordinator, primary investigator and teacher of medicine. I have chosen to apply to medical schools where physicians with bold ideas are nurtured so that their dreams can take shape. What I seek is not unlike what I provided for three years to my students in Tanzania: a quality education built upon a foundation of caring and commitment. With such an education, I will be well prepared to serve my community to the best of my ability by expanding its access to medical care.

ANALYSIS

Gregory immediately reels us into his story, immersing us into the dramatic story line of Deo's medical complications. The narrative reads like a fictional folk story, and that makes it even more powerful, considering how this experience is reality for certain communities. He does an incredible job of juxtaposing his modern, American perspective as an educator with this community with limited resources. He shows how he respected the traditions of this Tanzanian community but also how he used his modern medical background to try to see if there were possible alternate solutions. This demonstrates to the reader that Gregory understands the nuances of culture and values but also stays true to his commitment to helping others to the best of his abilities.

Gregory excels at depicting how he connects with others, especially his students. His story of teaching others is inspiring, and his passion for helping those with fewer resources shines through. Through the story he tells, he implicitly shows us different characteristics about himself, which he then concretely describes in his concluding paragraph to make it clear to the reader who he is and what he values.

—Melissa Du

KYLE R. B.

Hometown: St. Louis, Missouri, USA
Undergraduate School: Private, Howard University
Major: Biology / Pre-Medicine
GPA: 3.96
MCAT: 29. PS: 9, V: 10, BS: 10.

ESSAY

Summers in the city were tough to bear. My internship at the Community Action Partnership's Human Development Corporation (HDC) burdened me with the task of recording "Family-need Evaluation" minutes. When underprivileged individuals, some recent immigrants, entered the office to demonstrate their federal aid need, their physical appearance reflected their standard of living as much as their documents did. It was emotionally tolling to record details illuminated during the interview when I could not escape the thought that many aspects of their health condition were hidden, and even took a backseat to the issues that my job attempted to resolve. Dr. James Whittico first exposed me to treatments that utilized a complementing clinical approach for human betterment. He allowed me to observe a remedy that my occupation's food pantry, energy assistance, and financial literacy provisions could supplement to improve our community members. Each day after work, I'd watch this past National Medical Association president surprise clients with his recollection of prior visit details and affectionate treatment. Dr. Whittico explained every encountered condition to me as if I was his colleague, and he inspired me to pursue a lifestyle in health care.

Guidance from my mentor amplified my interest in science courses. On alternating days during high school, between my final class and evening sports practice, I was either leading Science Olympiad exercises as co-Captain or further examining my Anatomy & Physiology group's dissected cat. My AP Biology instructor required that every student summarize a research publication each month. Reading about scientific discoveries helped me to view the subject as a "living" field, and it stimulated my interest to unearth findings of my own. Violence among the middle-aged and child abandonment had left the "head of household" responsibility to most elderlies who entered the HDC. While the education background and language barrier sometimes justified clients' confusion during the interviews, there was often an unexplainable behavior of disorientation demonstrated. Conducting dementia research under the direction of Dr.'s Burke (Howard Univ. College of Medicine) and Lemere (Harvard Institute of Medicine) helped me to identify more Alzheimer's disease characteristics. Further studies on the physiological correlations with this ailment made me realize that a stronger grasp of biochemical pathways helps to promote treatment innovation, so I submitted my UK fellowship application to gain more preparation for service.

Contrary to the balanced-course US curriculum, Oxford offered me only classes that aligned with my Biochemistry major. Small group tutors who learned to recognize my tendencies, challenge me beyond comfort, and structure my progress with each meeting accompanied a typical institution's lecture theatre presenters. Unlike the familiar standardized multiple choice and short answer tests, Oxford evaluated me on the merit of my ability to connect multiple topics and to accurately incorporate mechanisms into the whole being through compositions. Each day spent assessing various system interpretations sharpened my eyes for identifying valid experimental evidence. I had no idea that even popular textbooks cannot always be trusted as the undeniable truth. One textbook and Wikipedia used to be sufficient for each subject. Now, I cited at least four textbooks, and many more current research publications, before providing my analysis for each paper. I have become so familiar with the respective focuses of each reference that I even recognize which one would best assist my response to certain prompts. Devlin's works must be consulted when I seek to uncover a corresponding diagnosis for protein deficiencies, while Stryer displays mechanisms with great clarity.

The fellowship year abroad taught me the basics of dynamic discovery that I will continue to utilize throughout medical training. By not limiting my resources, I plan to take full advantage of the medical education in preparation for a health care career. My pursuit of service through the clinical profession spawned from my desire to serve more effectively, and each subsequent experience leading to my destiny has further fueled this aspiration. Examining the Kenyan sanitation practices and creating a presentation with Swiss clinicians as a "Teach a Child—Africa" volunteer taught me the consistency of medical practice throughout the world. Of course, there is great importance in recognizing the culture-specific afflictions, but the surprisingly uniform translation of medicine alludes to an opportunity to serve both a local and global community. I am equally as intrigued by medical practice technique turnover through time as I am of its uniformity across space. Brigham and Women's Hospital surgeon Dr. Eldrin Lewis told me during my weekly shadowing session that everything studied 20 years ago had now become obsolete in his specialty field. I am thrilled with the need to be a lifelong learner, an open-minded caretaker, and a creative visionary. During medical school, I will develop skills that I practiced during bench research and distinct curriculum styles in order to improve the health condition of humanity, one patient at a time.

ANALYSIS

In this essay, Kyle relates the academic rigor he has honed through his undergraduate experiences to his desire to use this skill set to serve humanity through medicine. In particular, he goes into depth on a transformative fellowship abroad at Oxford. As he compares this to the United States, he demonstrates an inquisitive and reflective nature. In addition, he connects this fellowship experience with his prior experiences and internships, establishing a strong narrative that aptly describes his academic background.

Kyle effectively relates this academic dimension to his interest in medicine in the last paragraph where he clearly describes his desire to help others in a health care career. This motivation is well supported from the sentiment established in the opening and from specific examples of Kenyan sanitation practices and Swiss clinician presentations introduced. These latter experiences in particular demonstrate that he holds a cosmopolitan awareness that sets him apart from other applicants.

Kyle concludes with a powerful sentence that reflects his desire to continue impactful learning that will improve the lives of others, which is an important and recurring theme throughout the essay.

—Deni Hoxha

MICHAEL WU

Hometown: Edina, Minnesota, USA
Undergraduate School: Private, Harvard University
Major: Molecular and Cellular Biology
GPA: 3.94
MCAT: 42. PS: 15, V: 12, BS: 15.

ESSAY

Of all the doctors I had met, this one was by far the strangest, and I looked upon her with some suspicion. She was a sickly-looking young woman who could not have been much older than me, sitting on a dirt floor. She avoided eye contact as we walked in. None of these things did her bedside manner any favors, nor did the fact that her medicines were all stored in recycled Smirnoff vodka bottles. But looking around, I realized that this was probably what the practice of medicine had looked like for most of human existence. She was a healer in the original sense of the word, the sangoma of a Zulu village in the Valley of 1000 Hills, South Africa.

The first rule when one visits the sangoma is that one does not say a word. That is, not until she asks a number of questions which may seem mysterious to the Western ear. Do your bones hurt? Your son is strong? Your cows are fat? Your ancestors have spoken to you? A patient with a stomachache does not simply tell the sangoma, but rather waits and answers her questions until she asks if he has a stomachache. At this point, a cure can be devised. This roundabout way of diagnosis caused me to ponder the original concept of medicine. It also made me look back on the path that had brought me here in the first place.

When I arrived at college as a freshman, I eagerly looked forward to receiving a great education from the faculty and my outstanding peers. Little did I expect that I would learn just as much from the homeless people in front of the local CVS pharmacy. As a health resources advocate, every week I lead a team of volunteers to community dinners for the homeless and low-income residents of Cambridge, where we offer free health resource counseling and blood pressure testing. While we strive to help our guests obtain health insurance and find clinics, I've realized that one of the most valuable services that we offer guests is simply listening to them. For people who spend their days begging from strangers and being mostly ignored, finding a listening ear is therapeutic. And with open ears, I've learned a lot. One weathered-looking homeless man even quizzed me about the Krebs cycle and ATP synthase as I took his blood pressure, just in time for my upcoming exam. The seemingly one-dimensional profile of a low-income guest with a health problem is actually a complex 3-D narrative, full of social factors, anecdotes, and even fun facts. I sometimes wonder if this 3-D view of a person was something that the sangoma's holistic questions were getting at.

The sheer simplicity of the sangoma's hut also reminded me of one of the moments that touched me the most while shadowing physicians. While I have glimpsed medicine at some of its more dramatic moments, such as observing treatment of a patient with a life-threatening bone marrow infection, I have also seen its more mundane moments, watching a family physician patiently taking care of a patient's earwax complaint. And surprisingly, it was at such unglamorous moments that the humanness of the patient-doctor interaction struck me the most. I realized just how much goes into being a caring physician: not just medical expertise, bedside manner, and work ethic, but true commitment to care in even the little things, including but not limited to cleaning out a waxy ear canal. To me, this kind of commitment to care is what makes a healer.

If I found the sangoma's method of diagnosis intriguing, I wondered what she would have thought of mine. As a summer research fellow in the microfluidics lab of Dr. Frederick Balagaddé in South Africa, I was writing a computer program to help develop a small microfluidics chip that could serve as a point-of-care diagnostic platform for diseases like HIV and TB. As Dr. Balagaddé likes to say, we want to "fit 99 doctors into a chip," enabling multipurpose diagnostic testing in even the most rural settings. In this sangoma's village, most people had barely enough money to take a crowded minibus to the city clinics. But what if we could one day give that sangoma a user-friendly "lab on a chip" that could allow her to conduct several tests with a single device without ever leaving her hut? I find possibilities like this nothing short of thrilling and believe that this is also part of being a healer: envisioning a better way to deliver better care. My dream is to be a physician who not only gives compassionate care on an individual level, but also contributes to the translation of new discoveries in science and engineering into better patient outcomes in the clinic or the village.

When I think of the sangoma today, I am reminded of the fact that the art of healing is in constant flux, and that is part of the great excitement of medicine. I can't wait to see where the research questions of today take us, and how new understandings change the ways we treat patients. But I'm also reminded of the basic human commitment to care that defines and has always defined a healer, a commitment to care that I would be honored to be a part of. I can still see the dirt path leading away from the sangoma's hut today. It is long and winding, full of exciting unanswered questions, and I can't wait to get started on my journey. As I have learned, the answers often come from unexpected places.

ANALYSIS

Michael immediately captures the reader's attention by sharing his intriguing encounter with a sangoma. He compares the sangoma's caring and thoughtful approach to healing to his experience becoming acquainted with the homeless people he met while leading community dinners. In doing so, not only does he showcase some of his volunteer work, but he also effectively highlights one aspect of why he is drawn to the medical field: a commitment to care.

Michael moves on to discuss his summer research, connecting it to a desire to expand medical innovations and discoveries, highlighting yet another reason he wants to enter the field of medicine: the opportunity to make impactful medical advancements. By emphasizing his desire to innovate, he highlights his long-term goals as a medical professional and makes himself an even more appealing prospective student of medicine.

Overall, the success of this essay lies in Michael's ability to eloquently convey multiple experiences, both directly and indirectly relevant to the medical field, and then connect them to the core values that are indicative of his outstanding character.

—Katharina Wolf

Megha Majumder

Hometown: Plainview, New York, USA
Undergraduate School: Public, University of California at Berkeley
Major: Molecular Toxicology, Public Health, Sociology
GPA: 3.9
MCAT: 520. CP: 129, CARS: 130, BB: 131, PS: 130.

ESSAY

Most kids got a new car or the latest iPhone when they turned sixteen. My father bought me a book.

A book about death, really (as most everybody knows, he has quite the sense of humor): Dr. Paul Kalanithi's memoir, *When Breath Becomes Air*. It has achieved tremendous recognition as a moving narrative of a doctor's dying—rightly so. Unclasped, however, the book just happened to be an argument for an intellectually rousing way to live.

Dr. Kalanithi posited that the great divide between science and literature is false. That a life in medicine is essentially composed of—not merely ornamented with—the light and shelter of language. From him, I learned to draw on words to comfort patients. And now, more important to me than saving lives—in the end, everybody dies—has become the task of bringing patients and family members to an understanding of illness with which they might make peace. How else to do this but by speaking, and by listening?

At Berkeley, I saw how the humanities were so often positioned against the sciences. It broke my heart, so I devoted my nascent academic career to planing smooth the friction of their edges. This might be to the credit of Dr. Ann Swidler, under whose tutelage I began to conceptualize academic disciplines not as separate regions but separate vocabularies. When we see sociology and chemistry as vocabularies, we perceive that they are methods, not subjects, of investigation. Under unified examination across literature, the humanities, and the hard sciences: consciousness, living, the world.

In my time at Harvard, I began to be interested in other things besides science. My devotion to chemistry is still with me—I like its elegance and precision. It is simply that I have become aware of some of its shortcomings. Even my graduate studies in philosophy have come up short—it seems as though Hegel told us everything about the world except what it is to be a woman and to live and to die.

I hope that by following in Dr. Kalanithi's footsteps, I may find some truth to human experience—however perplexing and knotty it may be. What drives a young man to trade his ability—or his mother's—to talk in exchange for a few months of mute life? What renders this life worth living in the face of an otherwise tragic human mortality?

Every day, I grapple with this question, and to live, in my life, with a commitment to finding answers that I hope to uncover in the art of medicine.

ANALYSIS

Megha focuses on a character of intellectual discipline and well-roundedness. She opens with a discussion of a key milestone that shaped her personal philosophy: reading Dr. Paul Kalanithi's memoir. The insight in her analysis demonstrates her passion for the ideas in the book—in particular, the need to bridge the gap between the sciences and the humanities.

This segues smoothly into her own efforts to smooth that divide. She discusses her engagements at Berkeley with a professor to understand the nature of the gap and offer a glimpse of her own philosophical positions on the subject.

Megha elegantly concludes with an outlook on her ambitions for the future: to use medicine to answer the philosophical questions of life and mortality. The result is a character impression of Megha that shows that her intellectual curiosity drives her pursuit of greater medicine.

—George Moe

III. IMPACTFUL EXPERIENCE

ASHLEY SHAW

Hometown: Torrance, California, USA
Undergraduate School: Private, Columbia University in the
  City of New York
Major: Biological Sciences / Art History
GPA: 3.8
MCAT: 34. PS: 11, V: 11, BS: 12.

ESSAY

My interaction with "Sister" one afternoon in summer 2012 at Ter-
ence Cardinal Cooke (TCC), a 600+ bed skilled nursing facility,
imparted me with the gravity of palliative care at the end of life.
Sister was a Catholic nun who had served abroad, had a sharp
sense of humor, and loved Diet Coke. As for most of our medically
complex and disenfranchised long-term residents, TCC would
most likely be Sister's last home. I knew from talk of "Sister's decline" that she was imminently dying from cancer. One afternoon,
I discovered mail at a nurses' station addressed to Sister. When I
saw that it was two months overdue, I told the nurse that I would
deliver her envelope.

I arrived to find Sister in bed, thin and frail. Her nun's black
habit sat awkwardly upon her bare head. Sister could no longer
speak. I called her name and she slowly turned her piercing blue
eyes to me. I showed her the envelope and moved it into her hand,
asking if she wanted me to open it. Her look told me, "Yes." I
showed her the enclosed greeting card and $5 bill. I read it aloud:
"Dear Sister, my thoughts and prayers are with you. Here's $5 to

buy a Diet Coke." Sister did not move but she managed a small grin. I took her hand in mine and she held it with strength and warmth that defied her frail condition as she closed her eyes. Sister passed peacefully in her room the next week.

The thought that Sister might not have received her envelope before she passed tortured me and fueled my commitment to improve palliative care at facilities like our nursing home, where resources are stretched thin by falling reimbursement rates and other difficulties of our healthcare system. I see that the physicians and nurses are so overworked that they prescribe medication and monitor vital signs without always stopping to deliver mail to those dying in our midst. Dr. Anthony Lechich, our facility's Medical Director and my mentor, has always challenged me with this question: "How can doctors sufficiently address a patient's spiritual and existential pain in addition to the body's ills at the end of life?" Not yet a doctor, I searched for a practical and meaningful solution to help TCC fill unintentional gaps in palliative care.

My solution was to found the "At Your Service" volunteer program in my senior year. During its first year, thirty Columbia University undergraduate volunteers performed four hours of service each week in the realm of palliative care. They assisted in responding to call bells and keeping patient morale high on the units and during recreational therapy events. Each volunteer also spent two hours each week building a lasting companionship with a long-term resident with few family or friends. To date, my volunteers have read aloud "Sherlock Holmes" and "On the Road," played guitar, and shared conversations on politics and religion with their companions. Some accompanied their long-term resident until the resident's death. I am working during my gap year to solidify, improve, and expand on the program's first successful year.

At this time I can only hold Sister's hand and recruit student volunteers to accompany other dying patients but I hope to improve delivery of palliative care as a physician in the future. The physician plays a crucial role in making difficult decisions for their dying patients that can be, as Dr. Lechich describes, "literally life or death." Patients and/or their surrogate decision-makers base their end-of-life treatment decisions on the doctor's prognosis, which is more uncertain at the end of life than in earlier stages. Dr. Lechich has shared with me his frustration at how often physicians do not deliver a terminal prognosis in the delicate manner that lets the patient and their loved ones understand its uncertainty. Having shadowed such conversations at TCC, I have witnessed how a single conversation about prognosis and advance directives can make or break the trust between doctor and patient that is absolutely essential for effective palliative care and medically appropriate end-of-life treatment. In addition, only their physician can determine if a patient has "capacity to make his or her own medical decisions." Whether or not a patient has "capacity" may control their autonomy in how they die, especially when earlier efforts fail to secure those decisions for end-of-life treatment that will best respect a patient's own wishes. As is often the case at TCC, two concurring physicians share the responsibility of enacting advance directives for a patient without surrogate decision-makers when that patient loses "capacity." To do what is right by a patient at the end of life, a physician must master what my mentor calls the "art forms" of determining "capacity" and delivering prognosis. My time at TCC has shown me the increasingly urgent need for physicians to master the intersection of bioethics, medicine, and compassion necessary for attending to a dying patient. This need drives me to attend medical school.

I feel a powerful calling towards the unique ethical duties and decisions of the medical profession. For Sister and other patients dying in hospitals and nursing homes, and for all patients throughout their lives, I aspire to dutifully perform the physician's crucial role in preserving human dignity.

ANALYSIS

Ashley begins her essay with a deeply emotional and powerful encounter with Sister that enables her to recognize the troubling reality of palliative care. The encounter was a transformative experience for her, and she successfully conveys the frustration and profound internal strife it instilled in her. From there, she brings readers through her thought process as she ponders how she can leverage change and find a way to practically fill the gaps in care within her nursing home. Right off the bat, she demonstrates to be someone who is critical, aware, and willing to take initiative. She further impresses the reader as she describes her active pursuit to influence change in the nursing home by creating a volunteer organization that supports TCC doctors in filling these gaps. She provides readers with strong insights into her commitment to improving palliative care and her action-oriented nature.

Her final two paragraphs reaffirm her passion for palliative care as she expresses the responsibility doctors hold when engaging with dying patients. She demonstrates her careful and nuanced understanding of the complexities that must be considered in every interaction and then compellingly states exactly what she hopes to gain from medical school. Finally, she leaves readers with a powerful declaration as she asserts, "I aspire to dutifully perform the physician's crucial role in preserving human dignity," validating her as a promising candidate.

—Sabrina Chok

MARISSA LYNN

Hometown: Bow, New Hampshire, USA
Undergraduate School: Private, Dartmouth College
Major: Biology
GPA: 3.9
MCAT: 32. PS: 12, V: 9, BS: 11.

ESSAY

"You could say I'm on pins and needles," began my Korean co-teacher, Tara.

"What do you mean?" I asked. Tara passionately studies English in her free time and I've grown accustomed to her enthusiastic use of idioms.

"Pins and needles. What I want to say is I am anxious."

Around us, students and teachers gulped down bowls of noodles at lightning speed, without noticing Tara's distraught expression. I quickly forgot the steaming mound of slushy noodles on my tray. The cafeteria emptied as I listened intently to my co-teacher's worries and concerns.

"Remember on Monday, I said my son's fiancé's grandmother fell as she was leaving their wedding reception and went into a coma? Is that correct, went into a coma?"

"I remember and yes, went into a coma is correct."

"She passed away this morning."

This conversation occurred during lunch at the school I taught at, five months into my Fulbright Grant in South Korea. When I arrived in Seoul, I knew one Korean word, An-nyungha-se-yo, the formal way of saying hello. I feared isolation, loneliness, and confusion due to my inability to communicate. Sitting with my co-teacher in that crowded cafeteria, I realized we had formed a strong bond through our previous exchanges, which then allowed us to discuss a sensitive situation. I'd overcome some of my initial fears. Even though we lacked a common mother tongue, Tara had chosen to divulge a personal tragedy to me. Our joint vocabulary was limited, but expressions of concern, empathy, and sorrow share a universal language. Tara and I went from celebrating the joys of life—a wedding—to mourning the passing of a cherished grandmother. What profession is better attuned to the ups and downs of life than medicine? I possess a deep desire to understand and aid those around me, which has led me to pursue a career as a physician.

During my grant year, I've felt vulnerable when I couldn't express my needs, desires or opinions. I watched helplessly as a fight broke out in my classroom, as I could not communicate with the angry students. In social settings, I often become a silent bystander rather than an active participant—my voice is lost against an insurmountable language barrier. Patients can feel similarly vulnerable when discussing sensitive or frightening health concerns. How do you get a scared teenage girl to confide in you about her sexual activity or a stalwart grandparent to confront a gradual decline in mental acumen and possible Alzheimer's Disease diagnosis? Understanding their vulnerability and anxiety is the first step.

To dispel the nagging feeling of vulnerability, I have become proficient at relaying my ideas in the presence of a language barrier. The key has been developing patience and non-verbal communication skills. These skills will carry over to my career as a doctor. Every day physicians encounter patients who do not speak

English or who lack the ability to speak, and they must somehow forge a connection.

Beyond communicating, living in a Korean homestay has illustrated the importance of cultural sensitivity. From the use of proper greetings that compose an age-based hierarchical system, to dinner etiquette, to the collective decision making process that guides social conduct—I've worked to adapt and thrive under a new set of societal norms. Physicians encounter patients from a vast array of backgrounds and an appreciation for cross-cultural differences is critical for forming strong doctor-patient relationships.

Over the past year, I have embraced my role as a cultural ambassador—a hallmark tenet of the Fulbright Program. This critical responsibility is twofold: first to reflect a positive image of America and second to work to understand and embrace Korean culture. I have tried to present an accurate representation of America, but found it is difficult to portray the extensive range of cultures and peoples who make up our nation. I discovered it was best to take an introspective route and represent an America based on my experiences, not the America perceived by Koreans. While fulfilling the role of cultural ambassador, I was able to reflect on my roots, my experiences, and my beliefs. Such meditations have allowed me to connect my past with my goals for the future and will guide me as I prepare to enter medical school. This year it has become clear that a career in medicine will fulfill both my academic interest in biological systems and my desire to understand, communicate with, and help diverse groups of people.

The past year has brought a richness of new experiences, yet I always find myself thinking back to that moment in my school cafeteria. When the words left Tara's mouth, I hoped that she had misused the idiom. Tara opened up to me as a concerned mother, burdened with sadness, frustration, and disbelief. Such a level of personal confidence reflects a deep relationship formed through communication and cultural understanding. Our relationship spanned continents, generations, and languages. The few commonalities we possessed were mutual respect and openness. I know that as a physician, and as a person, these principles will guide all my future relationships—with my patients, my colleagues, and beyond.

ANALYSIS

In Marissa's essay, she expertly uses her life-changing experience teaching abroad to emphasize the importance of understanding patients' vulnerabilities and anxieties, communicating with patients, and accepting and appreciating different cultures.

She fluidly forges connections between each of these topics and lessons learned and experiences encountered in her year in South Korea. She draws parallels between her experiences as a teacher and the experiences of a physician. In doing so, she demonstrates how she plans to use critical lessons in communication, vulnerability, and cultural competency in her future career as a physician, validating her as an excellent candidate for medical school.

Marissa's excellent organization and clarity of thought throughout the essay add to the strengths of this personal statement. She is able to both implicitly and explicitly demonstrate that she knows exactly what it takes to be a doctor. The narrative introduction and focus on one central experience as a Fulbright Scholar keep the reader engaged and interested in her essay.

—Rebecca Lisk

OMAR ABUDAYYEH

Hometown: Kalamazoo, Michigan, USA
Undergraduate School: Private, Massachusetts Institute of
  Technology
Major: Mechanical Engineering and Biological Engineering
GPA: 5.0
MCAT: 38. PS: 14, V: 11, BS: 13.

ESSAY

I still remember witnessing the pain within my own family when my grandfather slowly died from stroke complications after losing his mobility and becoming fully dependent on others. I felt helpless through this experience watching the family doctor exhaust all options to save my grandfather's life. I wished to do something, but could not and so I began thinking about becoming a doctor. Later on through my numerous experiences, both clinical and in the community, I have become even more determined to pursue medicine since it offers a perfect balance between wanting to help people and my interest in science and technology.

Interested in exploring a career in medicine, I shadowed a cardiologist who still inspires me with his passion for healing through innovation and his affectionate nature with patients. He introduced me to angioplasties and the various medical devices he invented from novel stents to an automatic detector of heart attacks. He amazed me with his ability to develop novel technologies for enhancing the lives of many, but it was his heartfelt interactions with his patients that especially resonated with me.

Eager to see more aspects of medicine, I volunteered in hospitals and shadowed surgeons. My volunteering duties at Borgess Hospital in Kalamazoo involved delivering surgical tools to operating rooms which allowed me to view operations such as a C-section and open-heart surgery. My shadowing at Massachusetts General Hospital brought me even closer to surgeries. Especially fascinating was a recent case I witnessed of a 60-year-old man with esophageal cancer. I watched the surgeons wield their tools to cut through tissue with remarkable detail and accuracy while avoiding vital tissues. Bypassing the esophagus by connecting the mouth directly to the stomach astonished me—particularly how the anatomy of a person could be significantly altered and yet the procedure would save his life. I envisioned myself in the doctor's shoes, working hard for hours to save the patient's life. Excited by these experiences, I became more resolved to study medicine.

Part of why I feel drawn to medicine derives from my desire to help others. Over the past three years, I had the privilege of serving my dorm as a Medlink representative, an on-call link to medical treatment and advice. As Medlinks, we are trained by MIT Medical in first aid and CPR and are provided with an approved stock of over-the-counter medicines to administer to peers in our dorms. I vividly recall one Saturday night when a student came to me on the verge of tears with rashes on his arms, uneasy about an allergic reaction he was having to his dinner. Determining Benadryl was the appropriate treatment from a discussion of his symptoms and medical allergies, I administered a dose to him. In two hours, his symptoms cleared and he hugged me saying, "You saved me." For the first time I truly experienced how it feels to help someone in need of immediate care. We are now good friends, connected by a short, yet profound moment.

I have also had many rewarding interactions with underserved middle school students while serving as a mentor in several science and engineering programs for the past six years. Two Cantonese children I worked with on a projectile motion project at MIT, however, stood out the most over the years. They were recent immigrants with limited English speaking and writing abilities. Week after week, I patiently pushed them to scour books and the Internet, encouraging them to read literature and think of experiments to test. Despite my frustration at times, I was successful in motivating them to stow away doubts and fear of failure and to learn something entirely foreign. During their final presentation, I could see the excitement radiating from them, filling me with a sense of satisfaction from knowing that I was able to help.

Aside from reaching out to the community, research has been a significant part of my life outside the classroom for the past five years. I once presented my work on the anatomical investigation of neurons on a local access cable network. After the show, one of the cameramen approached me and enthusiastically shook my hand, talking to me about his daughter's neurological disorder. He understood my presentation as he spent months researching neurological diseases and investigating treatments. He thanked me for working hard to better the understanding of the nervous system for the sake of people like his daughter. Thinking about our conversation, I knew my career would have to involve helping people through both research and medicine.

Knowing that I am pursuing a challenging career, I am confident that I will be able to use the skills I mastered in many aspects of my life, such as my rigorous education, volunteering, mentoring, and research experiences, towards treating patients and contributing to medicine. While feeling helpless through my grandfather's sickness initiated my interest in medicine, my ensemble of experiences and my passion for science and engineering have brought me to pursue medicine where I can wholeheartedly give and be part of the profession I so admire.

ANALYSIS

Omar explains how his strong interest in helping others draws him to medicine. He opens the essay with the painful personal experience of losing his grandfather, which he frames as the spark for what inspired him to become interested in becoming a doctor. From this experience, he then outlines the path that he followed to discover more about the field. He shows how he has grown from hardship, taking initiative so that he no longer feels helpless. The detail with which he describes the operations he observed makes it clear that he is fascinated by surgery.

For Omar, the personal relationships and interactions he makes with his patients are what makes medicine so meaningful. He exemplifies this by describing experiences directly related to medically treating others as well as experiences where he mentored underserved children. Through this breadth of experiences, he shows the reader that he is not only truly dedicated to serving others but also a well-rounded candidate, who has both the hard and the soft skills to thrive in medicine. That he addresses advanced surgeries, allergic reactions in his college dorm, and service to middle school students with the same urgency and passion demonstrates that he has what it takes to become a doctor.

—Evelyn Manyatta

Selena Li

Hometown: Sacramento, California, USA
Undergraduate School: Private, Harvard University
Major: Molecular and Cellular Biology
GPA: 3.97
MCAT: 39. PS: 13, V: 12, BS: 14.

ESSAY

"Foot Care," "Condoms," "Yeast Infection Kit." I squinted to read the labels as I restocked the medicine cabinet in the basement of Harvard-Epworth Church. An unpleasant fusion of body odor, tobacco, and artificial grape threatened to overwhelm me. It was my first day as a volunteer with Youth on Fire (YOF), an organization that provides a range of services for at-risk youth in Cambridge, including food and hygiene supplies, needle exchange, and overdose education. Because many of our program members are intravenous drug users and sex workers, we also seek to offer counseling and limited health care. As I went to fetch more spray-on deodorant for this eclectic collection labeled "medicine," I began to ponder what this label really meant to me and how I ended up here.

Early on, I understood medicine to be an extenuation of biology, a field of discovery and intellectual prowess. As a child, I discovered a fascination for science when I was six years old, exploring my backyard with my first microscope set. After exhausting the slides provided, I created my own with leaves, insects, and hair. This curiosity developed into a knack for biology in seventh grade when I was lucky enough to dissect a fetal pig. As a hobby blossomed into a potential vocation, I entered the world of research my freshman year of high school, enjoying every moment of designing experiments and analyzing results. Convinced that medicine meant understanding biology, I shadowed, researched, and studied physiology for leisure. I thought about cellular respiration during swim practice ("I'm tired . . . I must be running out of ATP!") and mentally traced the route of the digestive tract during dinner. I even attempted to diagnose my occasional stomach pains and examined my own sore throat with a flashlight and mirror to look for symptoms of strep. At the beginning, I fell in love with medicine because of a fascination with the natural world and a hunger for knowledge.

When I came to college, I realized a more visceral affinity for medicine when I attended a surgery seminar with the Harvard Premedical Society. I remembered this mixture of excitement and calm coming over me as I learned to insert a neck catheter. With an ultrasound wand in one hand and a needle in the other, I felt at home as I located the central vein on the simulation dummy. I let out a slow breath and smoothly inserted the needle. Blue liquid rushed into the catheter, affirming my success. In this instance, I knew that medicine was no longer restricted to my mind, but instead, permeated through my entire body as a physical, hands-on experience. However, even then, there was still something missing from my understanding of medicine.

Oddly enough, it was not during an exciting surgery or successful experiment but during an average night in my dining hall that I found this missing piece. I was browsing the portfolio of one of my favorite photographers, Chris Arnade, and found his new series, Faces of Addiction. This photojournalism project followed the lives of prostitutes and drug addicts in Hunts Point, New York;

Impactful Experience

in the next four hours, I met Millie who died from an overdose, Michael who sometimes became Shelly, and Eric who had dreams of getting clean and owning a farm. Reading their life stories, I realized that perhaps the idea of temptation, relapse, and redemption might not be that foreign. I looked upon those misunderstood faces and didn't see drug addicts. I saw humans whose coping mechanisms may differ, but who have fears, make mistakes, and require grace just like me. Though I had not experienced drug addiction myself, I found myself relating to this group, and the pain of feeling their suffering would not leave me. I now knew that medicine was not only intellectual and practical, it was understanding. Regardless of one's history, mistakes, or beliefs, medicine touches upon the very essence that makes us human and allows us to care for others as our peers.

Beeeeeeep. The ring of the doorbell jolted me from my thoughts. As I glanced at the monitor, I saw a woman with a mop of dreadlocks and bright red sneakers. That day I met Sal, an African-American transsexual whose drug of choice was heroin. I helped her pick out some new socks from our hygiene cabinet and heat up beefy mac and cheese from the pantry. She challenged me to a game of pool and won.

The truth is that while the exhilaration and intellectual rigor of medicine first drew me to this field, there is something deeper, almost unexplainable, which allows me to say with full certainty that this is my future. While I still feel the rush of excitement when conducting physicals or thinking through differential diagnoses, I also feel the warmth and complexity of a person's character, the bitterness of their afflictions, and their need for healing. When I think about medicine today, becoming a physician is no longer the end goal, but a way to best equip myself. I joined YOF to serve despite my limited skills today, but I know that with a medical education, I will be poised to do so much more for so many more.

At the end of the day, I brought Sal to the medicine cabinet, hoping that one day, I could offer her more than just "Foot Care," "Condoms," and "Yeast Infection Kits."

ANALYSIS

Throughout the essay, Selena delineates the development of her passion for medicine from an academic interest in biology to an excitement for its practical applications via hands-on experiences to her ultimate appreciation for the human aspect of the field.

Selena uses a powerful anecdote to illustrate a transformative moment in her life that invigorated her passion for medicine. She recalls looking through a photography journal of "the lives of prostitutes and drug addicts," recognizing how misunderstood the people featured were, and realizing that humans are complex beings. She effectively uses this anecdote to segue into the reasons why she is interested in a career in medicine, like the opportunity to understand and help people, particularly those who are often misunderstood.

By explaining the varied unique circumstances that drew her to the medical field, Selena communicates an enthusiasm to help and an admirable appreciation for often-overlooked patients that makes her stand out as an applicant.

—Katharina Wolf

JANE MILLER

Hometown: Woodstock, Connecticut, USA
Undergraduate School: Public, The United States Military
  Academy
Major: Life Science
GPA: 3.94
MCAT: 514. CP: 128, CARS: 128, BB: 129, PS: 129.

ESSAY

One afternoon, when I was fourteen, I came home from school, tossed my backpack on the couch, and shouted for my Mom. "What's up?" she called back. She did not expect the next words out of my mouth to be, "You will never guess what I learned about the mitochondria today!" She burst into laughter—here was her teenage daughter, raving about the mitochondria rather than the *Seventeen* magazine sitting on the coffee table. This deviation from the standard interests of teenage girls was not surprising—both of my parents are veterinarians, and I grew up surrounded by science and medicine. I used to comb through the *Journal of the American Veterinary Medical Association*, even though I inevitably ended up looking at the pictures of the strange household objects that gluttonous dogs had swallowed. I yearned to comprehend the print on the pages, but as a child, understanding the science behind these articles seemed like a lofty goal. Finally, in high school biology class, it started to click. I began to understand biology as the complex subject it was, and I was ecstatic. The lesson on mitochondria ignited my passion for science—how could these tiny organelles power and enable such a diverse spectrum of cell types?

Initially, I planned to attend a civilian undergraduate college. During my junior year of high school, however, I felt I had a second calling: the U.S. Army. I researched careers as an Army doctor and spoke to a handful of physicians and career Army officers. In particular, my uncle, COL (R) Christopher Toomey, and I discussed the realities of a career in the military and his experience with Army physicians. During multiple deployments, he had experience with many doctors. Rather than discourage me, his frank discussions about Army Combat Support Hospitals and the doctors and nurses who work in them only strengthened my resolve to pursue a career as an Army physician. As I progressed in my classes at West Point, however, I began to have doubts. I had many options to pursue, such as becoming a platoon leader or going into research. How could I be sure that I wanted to practice medicine, and that pursuing medicine fit the Army's needs? My West Point experience has illuminated that my role is to ensure the health and welfare of soldiers. In particular, my experience as a Cadet Team Leader showed me the importance of ensuring soldiers are healthy and cared for while they train and prepare for their future missions. The responsibilities of a Team Leader are to ensure the health, welfare, and success of a single freshman.

As a sophomore Team Leader, I was responsible for the sweetest, but most frenetic, young woman I have ever met. She was overwhelmed by West Point and the rigorous course load. Early in the semester, I got a phone call—my frantic freshman had needed advice over something quite minor, and called me for help. I was studying for a big Organic Chemistry quiz and told myself I would only go up to her room for a moment. When I opened the door, I immediately noticed the red puffy eyes of my freshman, who was curled up in her chair with a box of tissues, too overwhelmed to work. I forgot about the quiz—I had to, because I had a soldier in need. We talked for hours and, finally, the tears stopped. Moments such as this one occurred many more times throughout the semester, but she was thriving as a Cadet by the end. When I became a Cadet Platoon Sergeant and became responsible for more cadets, I spent even more time tending to the needs of my subordinates. These experiences helped me realize my desire to dedicate my career to improving the physical and mental health of soldiers.

While my passion for science has motivated me to pursue medicine, it is really the experiences with the people at West Point that have clearly showed me that being a doctor is my duty. Sometimes when I look around at my classmates, I think about how desperately I want all of us to make it to our fiftieth, tenth, and even just our five year reunion as we navigate a dangerous profession. It hit me that there has to be somebody to bridge the gap between battlefield wounds and stateside healing. My roommates have caught me sleeping curled up with my Human Physiology textbook. My friends tease me for my Organic Chemistry "artwork" that covers the study room's whiteboard. However, they have no idea that they are all the primary motivation for my hard work. I can only hope that my small role would help bring a soldier home safely or be able to get back in the fight. While my friends tease me for making them listen to my speech about how fascinating the mitochondria is, perhaps this is why the mitochondria is my favorite organelle; I appreciate how such a small organelle has dedicated its entire existence to the rest of the cell's survival. Similarly, I see myself as dedicating my profession, and all the energy I have, to these remarkable people that I have been blessed to know. The men and women who have dedicated themselves to service are all somebody's battle buddy, spouse, or child, and they deserve somebody who will go the extra mile as their physician.

ANALYSIS

Jane primarily focuses on her experience as a leader in the United States Military Academy. This close-up of her role as a Cadet Team Leader illuminates how much she values serving others, both on the macroscopic scale of the United States but also on a more personal level, with her cadets and fellow soldiers. As she walks us through her journey of choosing where she wanted to go to school to ultimately becoming the leader of her own team, she shows us how she has matured and discovered what she truly values. This proves to the reader that Jane will be a great doctor, as she dedicates herself to helping others so that they can succeed, rather than focusing on just herself.

Looking at her essay more structurally, Jane introduces her essay with an anecdote about the mitochondria and references this anecdote in her conclusion as well, which wraps up her essay nicely. She gives personal meaning to the mitochondria, and the extended metaphor that she draws between herself and the mitochondria further reinforces how she is passionate about helping others.

—Melissa Du

EMMA MEYERS

Hometown: Englewood, New Jersey, USA
Undergraduate School: Private, Columbia University
Major: Neuroscience and Behavior
GPA: 4.0
MCAT: 35. V: 10, PS: 11, BS: 14.

ESSAY

"Have a minute to go over this follow-up? It was a tough one."

I spun around in my chair to face the intern helping me check in on patients a year after their strokes. She looked nervous.

"Sure," I said, mustering some degree of authority. It had been only a month since I began working at the hospital, and I was still getting used to having students not much younger than myself look to me for guidance, especially when they wore such concerned expressions.

She had called Mr. H, who had suffered a brain hemorrhage the year before, and spoke to his teenage son, who explained that he was worried about his father. Mr. H was finally feeling well enough to take care of things around the house, but he still wasn't able to go back to work. Instead of celebrating the gains in his recovery, Mr. H spent the better part of the day in bed, sad, fatigued and listless. Once he got on the phone, Mr. H told the same story: he felt useless, and the need to care for his children was the only thing keeping him going. He divulged suicidal ideation, and hinted that he had a plan.

"I didn't know what to do," the intern said. She looked at me nervously.

I nodded, trying not to look as uncomfortable as I felt. "I'll take it from here."

I don't remember exactly when I decided I wanted to be a doctor, but I know that I was young, that I was certain, and that I never looked back. Medicine, as far as I was concerned, was an elegant logical exercise with a tidy solution: you go to the doctor when you're sick, she figures out what's wrong, and makes you better. The intricacy of the human body was endlessly alluring, but its pathology existed in a vacuum. In many ways I'm lucky to have had this compartmentalized perspective; it's the product of a pure reliance on intellect, naïveté, and an upbringing free from serious illness. I was the kid who when asked why she wanted to be a doctor skipped "I want to help people" and answered, "Science is cool!"

By the time I was in college I had gained some insight into the more nuanced implications of illness. It dawned on me in an embarrassingly delayed fashion while working in a nephrology lab collecting samples from clinic patients that not only is it awful to be on dialysis but that needing it every other day for essentially forever is all-consuming, and one's entire life falls victim to the failure of two tiny organs. Volunteering at a neighborhood hospital in New York City was even more eye opening. There, where I could directly interact with patients and hear stories of how one's inability to conceive was hurting her marriage and how another's hysterectomy stopped her near debilitating pain, I began to learn to take to heart all the strains illness places on normal life. It seemed challenging to manage patients in ways compatible with their life values. In those physicians who were successful, though, was a willingness to look beyond the obvious answer. They made an effort to work with patients to determine if dialysis is the right option, or to choose the contraceptive most compatible with her lifestyle, and in doing so, they made the greatest impact. Their comprehensive approach stood out to me, and I knew it was a practice I wanted to emulate.

Now Mr. H was forcing me to evaluate the big picture myself. After half an hour, my frantic attempts to dial and redial every number in his chart were proving futile. As tempted as I was to give up, when afternoon turned to evening an uneasy feeling set in. I knew what my last recourse had to be.

"This is 911, what is your emergency?"

A social worker reassured me that ethically and legally calling the authorities was the proper course of action, but I still felt nervous and vaguely absurd as I described the situation. Sitting there on the phone, awkwardly explaining that no, I did not know if Mr. H was home right now and that yes, I understand that EMS might have to break down the door, it hit me how real this was, how it required action and how fast I was making decisions and how directly those decisions might impact the capital L Life of a person struggling with the effects of his illness. Sickness is big, I realized as I hung up, envisioning an ambulance wailing toward a stranger's home, and we need to be mindful of the whole spectrum of its effects.

Mr. H's depression going unnoticed showed me how easy it is to forget to see the patient as more than the composite of labs and scans. With a few pointed questions anyone might have diagnosed him. Addressing his plight taught me how a little consideration and a holistic approach can be life changing.

The scientist in me chose medicine because I found some notion of profundity in correcting nature when it goes wrong, some nobility in preserving life; all the rest was saccharine fluff. Now, I see there's no difference. The body does not exist in isolation;

when we treat it, we implicitly impact every other domain of a patient's life. Knowing this, I want to pursue the real crux of medicine: integrating the science of the body with the circumstances of patients' lives. This communion of elegant biology with the messy realities of humanity, the convergence of two sides of life, is where the true nobility of medicine lies. It is the greatest thing to which I can aspire.

ANALYSIS

The strength of this essay lies in its engaging narrative structure that draws the reader in while simultaneously communicating Emma's values, personality, responsibility, and clear thinking when under pressure.

Emma begins the essay with dialogue to orient the reader to her role at the hospital, then goes on to expertly weave in descriptions of her childhood love of the scientific side of medicine and her gradual realization of the devastating impact of illness on human life while working at the nephrology lab. She strikes an elegant balance between the spotlighted anecdote and her own personal reflection and effectively conveys the significance of the experience to her relationship to medicine.

The essay climaxes at the realization that her interest in medicine is not purely scientific, but rather very human in nature and dependent on the circumstances of the patient's life. By making the crux of the essay this realization, Emma successfully portrays herself as analytical and investigative and simultaneously thoughtful and compassionate, both in her past job at the hospital working with Mr. H and in her future as a physician.

—Rebecca Lisk

Larisa Shagabayeva

Hometown: Brooklyn, New York, USA
Undergraduate School: Public, CUNY Hunter College
Major: Chemistry II: Concentration in Biology
GPA: 3.79
MCAT: 515

ESSAY

When I was sixteen years old and about to become a high school senior, my father had an unexpected stroke: a Pontine Hemorrhage. The bleeding in his brain stem was severe, forcing him into a coma for eleven days. I had an incredibly difficult time understanding the magnitude of what happened to him. Besides controlled diabetes, he had no serious health issues so his stroke was completely unforeseeable. He had just returned from visiting my grandfather in Russia when he suddenly fainted in the shower and was rushed to the emergency room. As the youngest in the family, I had always been his little girl and missed him immensely while he was away. I was expecting to come home, hug him and hear about his trip. Little did I know that I would never have the chance to hear him speak again. I was actually finishing the last days of my summer internship at Mount Sinai Hospital when this happened to my father. During my internship, I met patients battling difficult illnesses but I never imagined my own family in a similarly desperate situation. Despite my uncertainty and fear, I found courage in remembering the many obstacles my family and I had already overcome.

I come from a home that lived the plight of many immigrants, from struggling with language and cultural barriers to dealing with financial problems. Having experienced such difficulties, I always honored education as my main priority. Most of my inspiration came from my mother who, at only twenty-seven years old, packed her life and hurriedly left Russia with my father and three young children to settle in New York. With minimum English, she passed the exams necessary to re-evaluate her nursing license from Russia. Before she became the superhero that I know, she battled strong anti-Semitism in Russia, which denied her certain rights such as entry into medical school. Her passion for medicine inspired me to learn more about science and her triumphs taught me that with hard work I could aspire to become anything I want to, especially with the freedom I was given in America. I wanted to learn more and applied to Mount Sinai Hospital's summer Hospital Placement Program for high school students. I shadowed an anesthesiologist in the two to three surgeries that I witnessed each day and once even saw a human heart beating during an open-heart procedure. I was standing at the forefront of medicine, discovering all of its beauty and how far it had advanced in helping people. However, I did not connect with the emotional side of my career choice until after my father had his stroke. In that moment, I was convinced there was nothing else in the world I wanted to become other than a physician.

I fell in love with medicine, feeling inspiration in the ability of a physician to shine a light of hope through the pure act of caring enough for patients' lives in their darkest moments. I had a small taste of that gratifying feeling when I cared for geriatric patients in Mount Sinai Hospital's emergency room. I felt privileged to be involved in and influence someone else's care, even if it was in the smallest way. At both Mount Sinai and at Memorial Sloan Kettering, where I did clinical research in the neurology department, the teamwork and leadership that I observed was unmatched by anything I had seen outside of the medical field. I remember the admiration I felt for my mentor's delicate manner in leading an end-of-life discussion with a family of a young patient dying from an incurable brain tumor. I was awed by her leadership in directing the conversation with a family stricken with grief, advocating for her patient's quality of life despite much resistance. I was also impressed by the way her team of fellows, residents and nurses supported her through this difficult challenge, much like a team of sailors hoisting the captain through the dread of a heavy storm. They helped answer the family's questions and used their own expertise to reassure my mentor that their ultimate decision for the patient was the right one. I also loved the creative thought process I witnessed when details of radiographic imaging and blood work were mapped to finalize a diagnosis and treatment plan. I could see myself in my mentor's shoes, plowing through all odds to help my patient, even through tough decisions relating to palliative care.

When my father had his stroke, I struggled to understand why medicine could not restore him to the undefeatable person he used to be. The damage to his brain stem was obviously irreversible but, after spending a whole summer witnessing surgeries that practically "fixed" people, it was nearly impossible for me, at sixteen years old, to accept that he and life would never return to "normal." It is still painful to recognize that his only way to communicate with me is to open or close his eyelids to signal yes or no, but my own direct exposure to medicine has helped me to come to terms with this. Having observed many interpretations of quality-of-life, I came to realize that although my father would not recover, he could still live out the rest of his life as joyfully and comfortably as possible with the help of his doctors, nurses and my family. Although I know the road is a long one, I feel excited to honor my father by embarking on a journey of constant learning, improvement and giving through medicine.

ANALYSIS

Larisa chooses to begin her essay with a difficult but life-altering moment in her life: her father's stroke. The impact it has on her becomes evident as she writes: "I was convinced there was nothing else in the world I wanted to become other than a physician." It is in this pivotal emotional and personal moment that she furthers her commitment and love for medicine.

The theme of Larisa's father's stroke continues to play out throughout the essay, but she does not lose focus of herself. Rather, she successfully delivers a compelling narrative that shows how his stroke has enabled her to view medicine in a different light and to further appreciate and admire the role doctors play in the patient experience. As she redefines for herself what it means to be a physician by drawing on her variety of experiences and mentors at Mount Sinai, she leaves the reader with a resonating portrait of not only her character and the values she embodies but also the empathetic and dedicated physician she hopes to one day be.

—Sabrina Chok

KATHERINE REDFIELD

Hometown: Tampa, Florida, USA
Undergraduate School: Private, Massachusetts Institute of
  Technology
Major: Mathematics with Computer Science
GPA: 5.0
MCAT: 35. PS: 12, V: 12, BS: 11.

ESSAY

Four years ago, I married my college sweetheart. Just over a year later, Sheldon was found without a pulse on the locker room floor at the gym. He was left in a medically induced coma with very low expectation of survival. For the next forty-eight hours, I watched over Sheldon's blue-tinged body feeling paralyzed by the weight of uncertainty. I have always been one for plans. And about ten backup plans. None of my plans accounted for cardiac arrest. I was overwhelmed with relief when Sheldon first opened his eyes after being brought out of the coma. I was then devastated when his breathing tube was removed and his first rasping words to me were, "Thank you, Nurse Amy." As my face fell, he grinned and said, "Just kidding, I love you, Kat."

  We celebrated his recovery and tried our best to return to normal life, yet it was clear our lives had been fundamentally changed. Until then, my intellectual and emotional pursuits had always been separate. I went into finance because the smartest and most interesting people I knew were going into the industry, and I sought meaning elsewhere. I built my career at Coatue, a well-respected, Manhattan-based hedge fund. My team of five created all the internal software tools required to run a billion dollar business. I enjoyed the company of intelligent, driven peers, mentally thriving under the competence they demanded of me. Meanwhile I spent my nights and weekends on activities that fulfilled me on a more personal level. I took dance lessons. I went hiking and camping. I volunteered at an animal shelter. I kept in touch with the students that I had tutored in college, continuing to assist them in their studies remotely. When those students went on to careers of their own, I co-founded an educational startup. I prided myself on my ingenuity in finding activities that fulfilled my emotional needs while allowing me to work a job that fulfilled my intellectual needs.

This separation of career and emotional interests had always seemed natural, until I almost lost Sheldon. The story of his tongue-in-cheek coma revival made him a minor hospital celebrity. I would watch the doctors move from room to room in the ICU with heavy steps, faces full of concern. However, when they entered our room, they were transformed. They practically glowed over seeing Sheldon's success. Doctors who had treated him, even briefly, made excuses to visit him, shake his hand and gush about how patients like him were the reason they had gone into medicine. It was inspiring and infectious to see how much joy Sheldon's recovery brought them. Suddenly I was surrounded by people who were smart, motivated and working on interesting problems they believed in. Their work was making the world, or at least my world, a better place. During these early months, as my research into Sheldon's heart condition took me to new intellectual and personal levels, I felt I had found a vocation.

Impactful Experience

I wanted to be meticulous and well informed about the approach I might take into medicine. To that end, I secured a computational biology research position at Memorial Sloan Kettering Cancer Center. There, I began bridging the gap between two careers: applying my computational skills to the problem of personalizing medical treatment. After confirming my interest in medicine through this experience, I began a program in pre-medical studies designed for career changers at Columbia University.

Remembering the vibrancy and excellent bedside manner of the staff who had treated Sheldon, I contacted his cardiologist and secured a semi-weekly shadowing slot. Through shadowing, I have learned the basic biology of the heart and, more importantly, formed a somewhat more realistic understanding of being a physician: the pros and the cons, the fascinating cases and substantial frustration of paperwork, the gratitude of patients and the pain of failure.

Dr. Singh specializes in treating adults with congenital heart defects; many are young, like Sheldon. Each time I walk into the clinic I see Dr. Singh throw his whole mind at a patient's problems. I find him trying to discover who a person is as much as what their symptoms are. I love that the overarching goal of "how can I make it better?" has as many social answers as chemical ones. I love that each patient is "John who just opened a coffee shop in Soho" as well as "John who just had a mitral valve repair."

Often, these patients have struggled with the specter of premature death for their entire lives. Their resiliency has given me a framework to think about the uncertainty my family faces. Despite his dramatic recovery, Sheldon's heart condition remains potentially fatal. Part of our treatment is accepting the things we cannot change. Part of it is enjoying the adventure of intentionally changing our lives. Part of it is cherishing the pieces of ourselves that remain unchanged: his playful teasing, our shared love of the outdoors, how I geek out over learning new things.

I have been coming back to the cardiac clinic month after month for two years. This experience, above all others, has soothed my planning mind and given me confidence that I am on the path to a career that feels exactly right: interesting, challenging and personal.

ANALYSIS

Katherine begins by sharing a personal story of her husband's medical case and how it impacted her. She immediately grabs the reader's attention in her shocking opening sentences. She continues to captivate the reader in her story by writing in a way that allows the reader to connect on an emotional level and vicariously experience the shock, helplessness, and relief Katherine went through. She reflects on this experience and explains how it played a pivotal role in not only her personal life but also her professional life. She takes the reader along in how her interest in medicine initially sparked, which helps to bring her application to life and show that she is a real and relatable person. By weaving together her personal experiences and her commitment to medicine, she retells an inspiring story of how she began her pursuit of medicine, conveying a genuine passion that highlights her promise as an applicant.

Katherine also elaborates on the measures she has taken to acquire knowledge and prepare herself for a career in the medical field. In doing so, she keeps the reader interested through her

Impactful Experience

narrative style while also showcasing her impressive dedication to medicine. This indicates not only that the medical field will be a great fit for her but also that she will be a great fit to the field.

—Katharina Wolf

FELICIA H.

Hometown: Placentia, California, USA
Undergraduate School: Private, Massachusetts Institute of
    Technology
Major: Biological Engineering
GPA: 5.0
MCAT: 35

ESSAY

My first exposure to medicine began with my aunt, an acupunc-
turist. I spent a lot of my childhood in my aunt's clinic "helping" diagnose patients. I became intrigued by this "magic" called
medicine—she pressed certain parts of the body to make pain disappear. Even as a child, I was perceptive of people's suffering—if
they were sad, I wanted them to tell me about it so I could take
some of the burden; if they were hurting physically, I wanted to ex-
tract their pain. No one deserved to be in pain. I thought medicine
could fix that. I saw doctors as heroes who sacrificed themselves to
help people conquer sickness and death.

As I grew, my view of medicine changed from a fantasized profession. I saw medicine as a protector when it rescued my dad from
prostate cancer my sophomore year in high school. I saw it as a
tyrannical force that dangled a carrot of a cure when my closest
aunt stayed with my family throughout her chemotherapy treatment for ovarian cancer. I saw it as a traitor when it seemed to sit
idly by as another aunt passed away from brain and lung cancer my
junior year at MIT. It was an ever-present force that guided some

people through personal challenges and brought out others' darkest insecurities.

My perspective broadened when I saw medicine deal with a tragedy that affected an entire community. The Boston Marathon bombings positioned me close to an emergency situation where I saw rapid medical attention on a vast scale. That day, medicine was a true north that allowed people to navigate their way when they felt lost and alone. But it also called for sleepless nights as doctors and nurses in the Boston area put their lives on hold to help. While the world saw the miracle of the survivors, I caught a glimpse behind the scenes, where the bombing took a heavy toll on the medical community. Medicine couldn't solve every problem; it couldn't make sense of the senseless violence.

There are, however, many real world medical problems just waiting for innovative technology to create a solution. I formed a team at MIT whose goal is to invent a portable, non-electrical IV warmer for trauma patients. The bombing validated the necessity for our device, which facilitates medical treatment on the field, whether in Afghanistan or in the heart of Boston. I've led my team in bringing the project from concept to prototype, where our next step is to finalize a field-ready product. Through this experience, I've discovered parallels between engineers and doctors—both are problem solvers. In medicine, a patient presents a puzzle of symptoms that the doctor must then decipher to reach a diagnosis. It isn't all about the final result. It's just as much about the creativity and challenging thought process behind the science.

Having always experienced medicine at the forefront of technology and treatment, I wanted to immerse myself in medicine's most raw form—without the hospitals and fancy equipment. I spent my last two winter breaks in Ecuador and Peru for MEDLIFE, volunteering at mobile clinics. The stark contrast between the medical facilities I was accustomed to from shadowing and the communities we served was astonishing. It was through this more personal involvement that I came to realize people aren't just puzzles to be solved; they are stories to be told.

One such story unfolded in Lima one day when I noticed a woman standing quietly to the side, as though something was troubling her. When I approached her, she responded in Spanish, "See the broken glass on the top of that wall? They built that wall to keep us out of the richest community, hoping we will disappear if they can't see us." When I stood by that woman, I suddenly saw through her eyes—medicine was an exclusive commodity she could never afford.

In South America, I was able to understand different cultures and relate to patients on a personal level. Whether it was consoling a patient who just found out she needed surgery or teaching kids how to use my camera, the opportunity to empathize with the patients, helping make their day a little better, allowed me to admire medicine beyond all the pure science. It wasn't all about the grand gestures; we weren't trained to treat patients. The small, unspoken things mattered just as much—that we knew they were having a bad day by reading their facial expressions, that we tried our best to understand their language and culture, even that we cared enough to play soccer with them knowing it would only embarrass us.

In reflection, I have tried to understand how, in a world of uncertainty, I absolutely know that I want to be a doctor. What began as an idealistic vision of doctors was transformed by how I saw medicine touch those closest to me. My perspective broadened as I learned the science behind medicine and saw it through the eyes of an engineer and volunteer. Through my experiences I have come to love medicine—flaws and all. It has become an intrinsic part of who I am.

ANALYSIS

Felicia explores her complex relationship with medicine throughout her essay. With anecdotes that explore loss and suffering of loved ones, she brings forth a very crucial point: medicine has its flaws and cannot solve every problem. Her change of heart from this perspective occurred after the bombing at the Boston Marathon, which helped her appreciate what medicine could do, amidst its imperfections. She unfolds in the following paragraphs her attempt to make the medical field more accessible and more impactful through her volunteer experiences in mobile clinics and her pursuit of developing an efficient warmer for trauma patients.

Overall, Felicia expertly communicates how, despite the flaws of the medical field, she is not discouraged—rather, she is motivated to find innovative ways to fill the current gaps. This demonstrates to the reader that Felicia is both passionate and a problem solver. With this nuanced understanding of Felicia's relationship with medicine, the reader understands that she is truly dedicated to making a difference in the medical field.

—Evelyn Manyatta

MELODY KING

Hometown: Warrenton, Virginia, USA
Undergraduate School: Private, Harvard University
Major: Engineering Sciences
GPA: 3.85
MCAT: 36. V: 12, PS: 11, BS: 13.

ESSAY

I was pounding on the treadmill when the call came. As I picked up the phone, my mother's calm voice came on the line. "I need you to come over to Margaret's now, she just collapsed and I can't carry her alone." My mother had left just a few minutes ago to chat with our elderly neighbor next door—something must have gone very wrong.

"Did you call 911?"

"Yes, but I need to move her to the front of the house."

"I'm on my way." I clicked off the phone and left at a sprint, charging up the stairs and out the door to Margaret's house. Barreling around the corner of her porch I saw Margaret had vomited blood across her entire chest, my mother struggling to drag her to the front of the house. I ran over and grabbed her feet. Up close, I could hear her gurgling through the blood, fighting for air with small, sharp gasps.

I felt utterly helpless. Other than sitting her up to keep her airway somewhat clear, I had no idea how to help. That was when I felt my priorities shift. I had previously thought I wanted to be a researcher, but that night I would have given anything—given up all the late nights I'd logged poring over biology notes and chemistry problem sets, the summers spent tanning under fluorescent light in a glycobiology lab—to know what to do. I realized then that, while I valued research and its promise of advances in the future, I found helping people in the present equally—if not more—compelling.

To be clear, I love the lab and find it immensely rewarding. Entering college I chose to study biomedical engineering over a "purer" science because I wanted to hone the creative, problem-solving mindset it teaches which is so invaluable to successful research. After dabbling a bit in biophysics and cellular engineering, I found my passion in micro-mechanical systems. It was exhilarating building a tool port for beating-heart surgery, or seeing a hinge I redesigned allow a tiny robotic honeybee to fly longer. Still, when I walked out of the lab, I knew my hours of modeling, prototyping, iterating and reiterating could maybe help someone in twenty years. For today's cardiac patients who don't have twenty years, open-heart surgery is still scheduled.

I got my first taste of what it means to be able to help people today as I prepared to lead a group of Harvard freshmen into the woods for a week. In training us to be outdoor leaders, the First-Year Outdoor Program heavily stresses competency in first aid. As I learned to splint legs with a backpack and check for spinal injuries, I only regretted I hadn't learned this five years earlier when my dad took a nasty fall as we hiked near the top of a 19,000-foot mountain. Hypothermia never crossed my mind as a complication of injuring his back. Knowing wilderness first aid could have saved us both a lot of angst, and him a bout of pneumonia. Though thankfully none of my FOP trips had an injury worse than a blister, I found learning first aid practical and empowering. I had learned something that made me able, if only marginally, to care for someone right now if they needed it.

But it was shadowing an engineer-turned-doctor that brought to life how fulfilling helping people today can be. I identified with Dr. Mansfield, an orthopedic surgeon with a warm smile and dry wit who had left his profession in electrical engineering because he "liked people more than machines." On an academic level, I was fascinated with his day-to-day work, from reading a confusing X-ray or MRI with the greatest of ease to constructing artificial joints for knee and hip replacements. But the personal aspect of the job was what seemed most fulfilling. New patients left with renewed hope, knowing their pain was being handled in a bearable amount of time. Veteran patients strode in confidently, able to sit and walk without excruciating pain. I even found myself comforted by his matter-of-fact descriptions of back injury healing rates, having just suffered a season-ending disc injury from rowing on our varsity team. He was helping people right now, independent of whether patent officials saw an innovation as novel or research funding sources fell through. And his main goal was never far from his mind. When telling me in between patient visits that herniated discs had a 95% heal rate in two to three years without surgery, the engineer in me asked what the point of doing surgery was in the first place. He simply responded, "You say that because you've never been crippled by back pain." After all, being a doctor is about helping people when they need help, not just analyzing the probability of success.

I want to go to medical school because, while developing better medical treatments and techniques is invaluable, I want to be able to help people now, as well—those who don't have time to wait for pills with fewer side effects or less invasive surgeries. So that one day, when another elderly widow collapses in her kitchen, I can do something to help her right then, when she needs it most.

Impactful Experience

ANALYSIS

Melody's potent introductory story highlights a shocking formative experience that brought their prior life values into question; their presentation of the helplessness they felt in the moment compellingly motivates their pivot from research into applied medicine.

Melody continues by reflecting on their nontrivial investment into research, originally set in place by their pre-college interests, and the satisfaction they found in it; then, by counterpointing this story with diversified experiences in "hands-on" application, from leading a trip in the First-Year Outdoor Program (FOP) to shadowing an engineer-turned-doctor, they show that college was a transformative experience for them and demonstrate how their education and experiences helped them develop and discover their passion for applied medicine.

The essay is eloquent throughout, written in a style akin to storytelling as Melody relates their path in life. The use of dialogue makes the experiences come to life and paints character into both Melody and the people and situations that have influenced them.

—George Moe

AMY MARTIN

Hometown: Massachusetts, USA
Undergraduate School: Private, Yale University
Major: Chemistry
GPA: n/a
MCAT: n/a

ESSAY

To be a physician is to be a leader. Deciding on a treatment plan when the diagnosis is uncertain; advising a resistant patient to follow the proposed course of treatment; directing nurses and other health care personnel in assisting in patients' care: these essential duties of a physician require leadership skills. Of course, leadership is crucial in other careers as well. What distinguishes medicine—and makes it my career of choice—is that it combines leadership with science and service in order to improve human health.

The importance of leadership in medical care was underscored for me while volunteering with Unite For Sight, a nongovernmental organization (NGO) that partners with eye clinics around the world to provide eye care to people living in poverty. I volunteered at Unite For Sight's partner eye clinic in Chennai, India, for two months last summer. Before heading overseas, I completed Unite For Sight's extensive training, covering topics from volunteer ethics to global health to cultural competency. I learned about complexities in global health work and strategies for addressing them. This training left me inspired and energized to be part of an effective global health program making a difference in patients' lives. Soon after arriving in India, however, I faced the reality of feeling limited in my impact. As a volunteer, I was restricted to distributing free reading glasses at eye-screening camps where ophthalmologists and optometrists from the clinic checked patients' vision and eye health. With medical training, I could have joined the clinic team in directly providing eye care, as well as offered the leadership necessary to raise the clinic's standards of healthcare to the best-practice principles I had learned about in my training.

By definition, leadership requires a group to lead. In medicine, this group consists of the medical team—including other physicians, residents, and nurses—as well as patients. I witnessed a physician-leader in action while shadowing a neuromuscular specialist at Yale New Haven Hospital during my sophomore year. Because understanding the patient's history and mental health is crucial to diagnosing and treating neurological disorders, my mentor spent about thirty minutes with each patient, talking about their personal lives in addition to their conditions and treatments. My mentor exemplified that having a caring and trusting relationship with the patient is as important a part of healthcare as prescribing medications and performing procedures. This relationship is essential for the physician to be an effective leader able to foster compliance in his patient.

I also enjoyed witnessing my mentor's collaboration with other attending physicians, his Neurology Fellow, Neurology residents, and medical students. I found their discussions of diagnoses and potential treatment plans to be mentally stimulating: it was problem solving as a team effort. The physician I was shadowing acted as a leader by respecting each person's contributions while making, as the attending physician, the ultimate decisions. My experiences shadowing cemented my decision to pursue a medical career, as I found my mentor's work enjoyable, meaningful, and intellectually satisfying. I am drawn to the diversity of interactions that medicine entails: those involving a physician leading a range of patients and other healthcare providers.

Finally, for a physician to be a true leader, she must make decisions with her patients' health as her foremost interest. As a volunteer in the Pediatric Intensive Care and Oncology Units at Yale New Haven Hospital, I have come to realize that being a healthcare provider is not about me; it should be entirely about the patient. I once visited a four-year-old boy who had a tracheostomy tube, which prevented him from talking and thus made communication difficult. After we had fun playing catch with his ball for a while, I understood—after some initial misunderstandings—that he wanted me to leave. I don't think I had done anything wrong; maybe he was just too frustrated with me repeatedly not understanding what he was saying. I realized that my purpose should be solely to make him feel as comfortable as possible, and if that meant entertaining him and then leaving when he had had enough, I shouldn't feel offended. Healthcare is about serving others, not oneself.

In closing, I am eager to enter the medical field, in which I will work as a member of a team in service of people's health and trust that I will emerge a leader.

ANALYSIS

Throughout the essay, Amy effectively brings together distinct experiences through the theme of leadership. She begins by explaining how medicine is attractive to her as the intersection of leadership and science. She elaborates how she came to appreciate this intersection, first through volunteering service abroad, second through a shadowing experience, and finally through a direct patient interaction. Throughout, Amy offers reflection on how these experiences shaped her value for the leadership dimension of administering medicine, noting in particular the techniques of her mentors that she found most effective.

These examples highlight the values she identifies with, namely the presence of team effort, development of a strong patient-doctor relationship, and prioritization of the patient. Through well-paced explanation of these aspects, this essay showcases Amy's understanding of what it takes to be a good physician.

—Deni Hoxha

TRAVIS BENSON

Hometown: Portland, Oregon, USA
Undergraduate School: Public, Portland State University
Major: Public Health
GPA: 3.99
MCAT: 515. BB: 131, CP: 128, CARS: 127, PS: 129.

ESSAY

I grew up in a small, coastal town on the Olympic Peninsula of Washington State. Port Angeles is a close-knit community that fits the cliche of the town where everyone knows each other. In 1990, my father came out as transgender. Being five years old at the time, the concept of gender identity was unknown to me. My father, who uses the pronouns they/them/their, was seen as deviant and psychologically disturbed. My family suffered as a result. The amount of discrimination my father experienced as a result of their gender identity was astonishing. Workplace discrimination left my family struggling to make ends meet on my mother's pay. Social discrimination alienated my family from the support structure we had developed in our community. Medical discrimination prevented my father from obtaining necessary gender affirming and routine medical care.

At the time, I did not have an understanding of why my father had to leave my hometown. I did not know the systemic discrimination that my parents faced as they attempted to keep their relationship intact. I did not know that my father was being refused care from their primary care physician. As I got older, I inquired about the circumstances surrounding my father's departure and health issues. My mother described the difficulty of getting medical care for transgender individuals. I learned about the barriers to care that the transgender community routinely experience. As a condition of treatment, my father was required to see several counselors; finding one that would even discuss their gender identity was a feat in itself. After receiving the necessary letters certifying that my father was mentally competent to make the decision to transition, they faced another barrier finding a physician that would treat them.

My personal experience having a transgender parent led me to research health disparities faced by the transgender community. I discovered that the experiences of my father were far from unique. Studies such as the National Transgender Discrimination Survey detailed the abhorrent amount of discrimination that the transgender community faces in a clinical setting. Further, I learned about the negative health outcomes that were associated with the lack of access to medical care. Physical abuse, depression, drug use, prostitution, and suicide were all associated with the inability to receive medical intervention. These findings hit me hard as I could see the hardships that my father and family faced in these statistics. At the same time, I saw these findings as an opportunity to improve the lives of the transgender community so that other people would not have to experience the same discrimination.

During my freshman year of college, I wanted to become involved in research that addressed transgender health disparities. I was not aware of the extent of the gaps in research regarding this topic. Without an established project to join, I decided to create my own research proposal and find a faculty member to help. My proposal was to conduct a health needs assessment of the transgender community in Portland, Oregon. Similar studies had been done in other cities, but not Portland, which has a relatively large transgender population. I found a faculty member in the School of Public Health who was eager to take on this endeavor and mentor me through the process. Community involvement in the development of this project was essential, which led me to become a member of the Oregon Health & Science University's (OHSU's) Transgender Health Program (THP) committee.

The THP had recently been established by faculty at OHSU and has been instrumental in increasing access and awareness of transgender-related medical care in the state of Oregon. I began attending monthly meetings, grand rounds, and town-hall events that were hosted by the THP. During this time, I met Dr. Aaron Ziegler, an Associate Professor in the Department of Otolaryngology, who conducted a longitudinal case study of a transmasculine patient who elected to forgo hormone replacement therapy due to socioeconomic reasons. Dr. Ziegler brought me on as a volunteer researcher where I conducted a meta-analysis on voice masculinization protocol for transmasculine patients. Through the guidance of Dr. Ziegler, I wrote a manuscript that analyzed the current clinical protocol and its shortcomings in addressing the communication needs of transmasculine patients.

Through the THP, I built relationships with several physicians who are active in providing gender affirming care. I observed the difference that these physicians make in the lives of their patients across a wide array of specialties; urology, endocrinology, internal medicine, family medicine, and otolaryngology. What I witnessed defied the findings of the National Transgender Discrimination

Impactful Experience

Survey. I found that, despite the social stigmas that surround gender identity, there are physicians and researchers who are actively
making a difference in the lives of this community. My desire to
become a physician was solidified by these experiences which have
inspired me to help improve the lives of medically marginalized
communities so that no one has to experience the discrimination
that my father faced.

ANALYSIS

Travis does an excellent job exemplifying his passion for medicine through a personal outline of some significant events that
led up to this essay. He begins with a pivotal event early in his
life when his "father came out as transgender" and describes his
recollection of the challenges his family had to face. What is so
incredibly powerful about his particular recounting is how evident his frustration is. He keeps his sentences concise and explicit
and uses the repetition of phrases like "I did not know" to build
the rhythm, momentum, and impact of his words. In doing so,
he effectively conveys the strong impression this experience had
on him and the close personal connection he feels to the issue of
transgender health disparities.

Travis continues to further impress as he describes how his
family's struggles inspired and fueled his passion for improving the
lives of medically marginalized communities. He writes about his
independently coordinated research project and his community
involvement in increasing awareness about these issues, among
other accomplishments. In connecting each of these accomplishments back to his family, he not only gives them additional weight

and significance but also demonstrates his strong sense of passion and initiative.

Travis strikes the optimal balance between personal narrative and measurable accomplishments in his essay and effectively shows how their relationship delineates both his interest and commitment to the medical field.

—Katharina Wolf and Sabrina Chok

GABRIEL MOLINA

Hometown: Gainesville, Florida, USA
Undergraduate School: Private, Harvard University
Major: Classics
GPA: 3.93
MCAT: 37. PS: 13, V: 11, BS: 13.

ESSAY

The door steadily opened, and she walked in with a big smile on her face and a bigger Polaroid camera in her hands. It was the first time all day that a patient walked in with so much excitement, and hers was of a special kind. In a room where everything was kept spotless and sterile, her excitement was contagious. I smiled back and introduced myself.

The 87-year-old woman named Linda sat down, placed her bag under her chair, and, still gripping the camera, extended her arms in my direction. "Could you take a picture of us?" she said and gestured towards Dr. Harrison. "I want to get a picture with the doctor who cured me of cancer."

Seconds felt like hours before, finally, Dr. Harrison calmly said, "That's actually what I wanted to talk to you about." She understood immediately. Her smile vanished.

In the moments before Linda's appointment, Dr. Harrison had given me a brief overview of her recent history. She had been a smoker for about 20 years before meeting Dr. Harrison. Shortness of breath brought her to her primary care physician; a large tumor in her left lung brought her here. She quit smoking, endured the long months of chemotherapy, tests, and check-ups and was cancer-free for a couple years. Her battle seemed to be over; she felt she had won. Her latest PET scan, however, was about to complicate the ending of her story.

Dr. Harrison appeared to shuffle in his chair as he leaned in and told Linda that her cancer had returned, this time in her right lung, but he was going to work with her once more to get rid of it. He promised that she would get a picture with the doctor that cured her of cancer, just not yet. It was clear that she did not believe him; she looked defeated. The first words out of her mouth were "I'm sorry," and she went on to tell Dr. Harrison that she had begun smoking again. She could not resist.

I was shocked. I could not believe that, after all the hardships, she returned to the one thing that had brought her to this office in the first place. I was frustrated by her decision and that it obscured my vision of her as an innocent victim.

It reminded me of how I feel when I am coaching and working with high school students to compete for a national championship in the classically themed quiz bowl–like game of Certamen. There is an underlying level of frustration that stems from trying to motivate kids to study and work hard when it is in their best interest and from losing patience when I seem to care more than they do about their own success. Earlier that week, I was quizzing and practicing with a few of the Certamen players, and it was clear to me that they did not study what I suggested. After all my time spent writing study guides and meeting with the students, it was tough to stay positive as I watched them miss questions we had just recently reviewed.

And yet I knew I would be back the next day, at the same time and place, ready to work with and for them again. The hope of seeing them heed my advice, gain confidence from my mentorship, take comfort in my experience, and use my resources to achieve personal success is always well worth the tireless effort.

So I sat and listened as Dr. Harrison navigated his way through Linda's desperate concerns. I learned that she had originally started smoking after her husband, a chronic smoker, died suddenly in his 60s. Smoking reminded her of him. Her house and bedroom regained its familiar smell and memories of the happy life she had with her husband bounced across the smoke-filled halls. Smoking brought him back to life, and she was addicted to his presence.

I watched as Dr. Harrison said just the right things and employed just the right kind of sensitive, yet deliberate, demeanor to instill in Linda the hope that she could quit smoking, beat cancer, and get that picture with him. In a mere fifteen minutes, he managed not only to educate and advise her on the path to success, but also to equip her with the confidence to begin that long journey. He vowed to be back the next day, at the same time and place, ready to work with and for her again. She trusted him; she was confident in him. More importantly, she was confident in herself.

Linda's seamless transitions from excited to dejected to hopeful, blanketed by a deep doctor-patient relationship, were shockingly familiar. They opened my eyes to the powerful roles of teaching, mentorship, and guidance in clinical medicine. These were the very same domains that brought me comfort, pride, and meaningful reward as a Certamen coach. That the Latin word "doctor" means "teacher" had never seemed more fitting.

From that point on, I saw Linda and heard her story whenever a student underperformed or understudied. She told me to be understanding, to withhold judgment, and to adapt and cater to the student's individual needs. She taught me that if I truly want to teach someone, I must first open my mind and be willing to learn from them.

The 87-year-old woman grabbed her bag, stood up from her chair, and, about to walk out, turned to me with outstretched hands. Her camera sat firmly in her palms. "Could you take a picture of us?" she said and gestured towards Dr. Harrison. "I want to get a picture with the doctor who's going to cure me of cancer."

ANALYSIS

Gabriel emphasizes the themes of empathy and guidance throughout his essay, framing the themes with a captivating narrative. He begins the essay by telling the story of a cancer patient who had recently begun smoking again. While at first Gabriel is disappointed to hear the news, he begins to see from her perspective and understand why she returned to something that had caused her so much harm. Gabriel effectively uses this anecdote to depict his change in perspective and his growing understanding and empathy, both of which are important qualities for a physician. By highlighting this pivotal moment in his life, he shows that he is capable of putting himself in a patient's shoes and communicating efficiently.

Gabriel also relates this change to his experience as a coach for high school students competing in quiz-bowl championships. He depicts his growth as a leader and his ability to "adapt and cater to

Impactful Experience

the student's individual needs," a skill that is directly relevant to a career in the medical field.

Overall, by choosing to focus on two specific events and showing how they altered his perspective, Gabriel highlights his personal growth as a leader that makes him an attractive applicant.

—Katharina Wolf

IV. IDENTITY

ROBERT WEATHERFORD

Hometown: Laramie, Wyoming, USA
Undergraduate Schools: Brigham Young University
  (Private), transferred to University of Wyoming (Public),
  post-baccalaureate premedical program at Johns Hopkins
  University (Private)
Major: English and Spanish
GPA: 3.98
MCAT: 35. PS: 11, V: 12, BS: 12.

ESSAY

I have not always known I wanted to be a doctor, romantic though it may be to say otherwise. As a young Wyomingite boy who spent his days roaming the vast expanses of prairie that were my backyard, I wanted to be an Egyptologist who worked outdoors digging up the ancient past or a veterinarian who traveled from ranch to ranch, vaccinating cows or delivering foals. It was not until my related curiosities about both the world of ideas and my fellow humans emerged as a teenager that I realized how nicely the vocation of medicine would pair with my developing interests. My favorite merit badge that I had earned at a Boy Scouts summer camp was First Aid, and I cherished my cheap microscopy kit for which I had scrimped and saved as a boy. By high school, medicine began to feel like a natural professional decision, and to that end I took a course to become a certified nursing assistant my senior year and continued my studies in science and math. I was naively but enthusiastically poised to begin my premedical studies at the university level and hoped that, with good fortune and perseverance, I would one day become a physician.

I also had the jejune confidence to assume that other aspects of my life would go according to my desires. As the fourth child of a Mormon family of nine, I had envisioned a very particular life for myself. I had always wanted to attend Brigham Young University, a private Mormon school in Utah and the alma mater of my parents and three older sisters. When I matriculated there as a freshman, I imagined completing my premedical courses, serving an evangelical mission like men of the Church were required to, marrying, and beginning a family of my own. Despite my strongest wishes, however, life had other plans in store for me. Doubts that I had long harbored in lonely silence about aspects of Mormonism—namely the long, racist history of denying the priesthood to black people and the blatantly misogynistic teachings about women—continued to rear their head in my life. After pensive reflection and assiduous investigation over more than a year, I ultimately saw the decimation of my formerly staunch faith. Also compounding my confusion at this stage of my life were my persistent feelings of attraction to other men, feelings about which I had been cognizant for years and that I had confessed to my parents at age 16. We all agreed then that therapy with a Mormon counselor and adherence to the principles of the Church would be the surest way to overcome these feelings, yet they did not subside despite valiant efforts. When I ultimately decided to leave the Mormon faith and transfer to a public university where I would be less encumbered by the academic and religious restrictions of BYU, the dream of medicine got lost somewhere in the tumult.

Medicine, however, was not content to be abandoned, and returning to my intention of becoming a doctor felt akin to coming home after an exodus away. It was auspicious to find that my meanderings in the interim between my original dream of becoming a physician and its rebirth years later had actually brought many unique gifts to my life to be used in medicine. First, my degree in English and Spanish and then the year I spent working in Spain as a Fulbright scholar honed my skills in both my native tongue and the language of the Latino community. It was my ability to speak Spanish that allowed me to work as an interpreter in a primary care clinic for the homeless in Portland, Oregon. There I was able to witness firsthand the power of medicine as a human service profession and to experience the joy of meeting the needs of those whose needs are often the gravest. Second, the process of accepting my sexuality as an indelible part of my being that is neither sinful nor pathological has helped me to understand people whose voices have also been dismissed or misunderstood. My longstanding interest in minority rights, coupled with my own experience of fighting for self-acceptance against cultural mores and years of indoctrination, have helped to galvanize my identity as a social activist, an identity that will inform the scope and nature of my medical practice one day. In addition to serving the Hispanic community at home and abroad and further developing my French skills to do international service work, I intend to continue my exploration of women's healthcare as part of my desire to address the needs of minorities. After designing and implementing a system of tracking cytopathology reports of Pap smears at the clinic in Portland and then shadowing a perinatologist for a year at the Johns Hopkins Hospital, my passion for women's health and wellbeing has increased exponentially, an interest which germinated many years ago when I first recognized gender-based disparities in my childhood religious community. In medicine, I will use my skills to advocate for, empathize with, and heal the disenfranchised.

All of my curiosity about how the world works and who the

sundry players on the stage of life are has continually been nurtured in my premedical education, both academic and experiential. I cannot wait for the chance to put my life experiences, passions, and quirks to good use in the vocation that I now confidently state I want to profess: that of a physician.

ANALYSIS

Robert begins his essay by stating he did not always know that he wanted to become a doctor, a rather uncommon statement that captures the reader's attention as well as sets up the rest of the essay. He explains how he initially became interested in the medical field as a teenager, whereafter he demonstrates tangible measures he took to pursue his budding passion, like becoming a certified nursing assistant.

However, he shows that his path to medicine was not a smooth one by discussing his doubts about aspects of the Mormon faith as well as experiencing confusion with his sexuality that ultimately led to his transfer to a public university. Parallel to this pivotal change was a distancing from his initial aspirations with medicine. Nevertheless, his passion for medicine reemerged, something he likened to "coming home after an exodus away." By showing how he came back to medicine despite some distancing, he illuminates just how special his connection to the field is.

Beyond establishing his unwavering commitment and passion to the field, Robert's personal experiences and knowledge of marginalized groups that have shaped him as an activist highlight his empathetic quality that would make for a great physician.

—Katharina Wolf

AZUCENA RAMOS

Hometown: Escondido, California, USA
Undergraduate School: Private, Smith College
Major: Chemistry and Neuroscience
GPA: 3.83
MCAT: 34. PS: 12, V: 11, BS: 11.

ESSAY

The year I turned seven, the words papeles and inmigrantes entered my vocabulary and settled on my family as a fog of dissonance between the American I was and the Americans my family members were not. That year began like any other with a huge family reunion and seemingly endless supply of Mexican food. Christmas had always been my favorite holiday; Christmas of 1994, however, opened my eyes to what being an inmigrante sin papeles earned you en los Estados Unidos. My grandmother, mi wita, nearly died of pneumonia after first contracting the flu. Without health insurance, legal immigration status, or a steady income, my family had little choice but to wait and hope for the best. It was then that I decided that I would not watch my family suffer like this without doing something about it. It was then that I decided to do whatever it took to become a doctor.

In my household where drunken beatings and verbal harassment by an alcoholic stepfather were common, mi wita was the most stable person in my life. Time spent with her was grounding, inspiring, and simply enjoyable. "Wita, why can't you bend your right arm? Why does the joint look so funny?" Unfortunately for my wita, she had grown up in a time where donkeys (who threw you off their back at whim) were the main means of transportation and medical attention was a privilege reserved for those residing in cities. The fact that she was able to raise 11 children while working in crop fields still amazes me.

More amazing was mi wita's demeanor. Despite a difficult life where she lost her mother to an undiagnosed disease and two small children to dysentery, where she endured crippling beatings from a cheating husband, and where food was always scarce, mi wita never demonstrated an ounce of resentment. Her loving nature, strong will and optimistic outlook make me proud to have been her niña. Losing her to pancreatic cancer this year has taught me to appreciate all that I have and to give thanks for every day that I am given. Most importantly, it has ingrained in me a deep respect for life and those who work to preserve it.

While almost losing my wita as a child is what first drove me to pursue a career in medicine, my mother's work as a nurse deepened my admiration for medical professionals. As a young girl, I joined my mom as she traveled to family, first in Mexico and then the U.S. I would watch her as she carefully loaded sterile needles with penicilina that my relatives had bought from Tijuana pharmacies, prescribed by doctores that looked like us, talked like us, and explained our ailments in a way nosotros Latinos understood. My mother also assumed primary responsibility for my wita at the end of her life. Serving people during their most vulnerable moments, my mother always demonstrated the utmost respect to patients and their families, teaching me how to provide care without being patronizing.

My mother's love for the medicine has always been evident, but then, so has the barrier to an American education and accreditation. This same barrier prevents her from doing what she

Identity

loves and, instead, restricts her to cleaning houses in order to support her family. My mother's inability to pursue her passion has taught me to take complete advantage of every opportunity that I am granted and has imprinted on me the added responsibility to work even harder in order to achieve success on behalf of both of us—on behalf of our entire family. Without my family's sacrifices, I would never have been able to graduate from high school, be the first in my family to attend and graduate college, and have the privilege of even considering a career in medicine.

My first opportunity to observe doctors came in the summer of 2007, during my time at the Summer Medical and Dental Educational Program at Yale Medical School. Here, I was able to shadow physicians in the ER and in low-income clinics. Being one of only a handful of program participants who spoke both English and Spanish fluently, the doctors were particularly thankful to have me around. I remember translating for a Puerto Rican stab wound patient and for a concerned mother whose baby was sick with pneumonia. And even as these exchanges begin to fade away with the tide of time, one image remains: the wave of relief that surged onto each patient's face after realizing that I was like them, that I understood them and could convey their fears and pose their questions to the doctors. Here, where I learned to talk to patients and their families, I saw how my heritage and our shared ancestry could bring immediate relief to my patients.

If helping the ill were my only interest, I would follow my mother's footsteps to become a nurse. I am, however, consumed by the desire to understand the science that makes us human, and especially about the brain. My interest in the brain appeared when my grandmother began to disappear, memories of her life and loved ones steadily stolen by Alzheimer's. Spending 2 years in a neuroscience laboratory cultivated my interest in research, so after college,

I followed my love for science into a stem cell laboratory. There, I learned what it meant to be part of a group that constantly works on high impact, cutting edge science. As cell lines and *Science* articles became integral parts of my daily routine, my vision for a career as a physician-scientist came into full focus.

My passion for learning and discovery is rivaled only by my love for helping others; practicing as a physician-scientist will allow me to accomplish both. I have experienced disparity firsthand and as a physician-scientist I will act as a catalyst of change, applying biomedical science to preserve and enhance the lives of those who need it most: people like my family. The day the cancer finally stole my wita I learned that no matter how much knowledge we possess, we are all inevitably mortal. Life is meant to be cherished, enjoyed, and lived to its fullest. My only hopes are that my life's work improves the quality of life of those in need and that every decision I make is in keeping with the advice my mother always gave me as a child, "You choose your future, mija. Don't let life choose it for you."

ANALYSIS

Azucena builds this essay around two influential women in her life: her grandmother and her mother. It is clear her grandmother's cancer inspired her to pursue medicine and her mother's love for medicine further sustained that interest. However, what is particularly powerful about her narrative is her skillful use of quotes and anecdotes as examples. She weaves informative snippets of her life into her essay and gives readers an authentic glimpse into her Mexican heritage and personal life. She also strikes an elegant balance between writing about those she admires and about herself.

Identity

In each description, she keeps her learnings and takeaways as her main focus and effectively provides readers with insight into her reflective and humble character.

Azucena continues her essay by describing a variety of experiences from her work as an impromptu translator to her research in neuroscience. However, her essay never feels rushed or disjointed. Each paragraph is concise and serves a distinct purpose in the essay, from demonstrating her understanding of diverse perspectives in medicine to highlighting experiences that inform her desire to become a physician-scientist. In her concluding paragraph, she links her goals for the future to her past with a strategic return to the influences of her grandmother and mother. In doing so, she not only brings continuity into her essay but also demonstrates her clear sense of direction and drive.

—Owen Searle and Sabrina Chok

SERGIO G. NÚÑEZ BÁEZ

Hometown: San Sebastián, Puerto Rico
Undergraduate School: Public, University of
Puerto Rico–Mayagüez Campus
Major: Industrial Microbiology
GPA: 3.9
MCAT: 508. CP: 126, CARS: 128, BB: 128, PS: 126.

ESSAY

A soothing warmth on my chest and a pervading smell of menthol—the memory that imposes itself on my thoughts whenever I recall the experiences that sparked my passion for medicine. Vicks VapoRub or "vi vaporú," as my grandmother Silvia calls it, was her first line of defense whenever I would catch a cold. Although in the end I always had to resort to more elaborate remedies to treat my maladies, it was not the complex mechanism of action of a pill, but my grandmother's earnest resolve to heal me that made me feel better, made me feel safe. This is just a simple anecdote, yet it was the seed that, along with my love of solving problems, impelled me into the path of becoming a physician.

Setting off from that childhood memory, I focused my undergraduate experience on breaking the mold that my ethnic and socioeconomic realities made me believe I had to conform to, all of this while my country dealt with crippling financial crises. I persisted even as my state-funded college education was placed in peril innumerable times by the threat of higher tuition costs and less infrastructure. I even pursued applying to medical school in my senior year and though my potential was recognized and I was invited to interview to several schools, in the end I was rejected. Through it all, I persisted and learned to see my failures and hardships as opportunities to pursue even further growth. I continued my personal and academic development by joining the Master of Medical Sciences in Immunology program at Harvard Medical School.

On September 20, 2017, exactly one month after I had left Puerto Rico, Hurricane María, a high-end category 4 storm, destroyed the island. The storm was the worst natural disaster on record for the island and caused the lengthiest blackout in American history. The aftermath of the hurricane continues to be more disastrous than its passing. As the hurricane unfolded, I had to witness in isolation as my homeland was leveled to the ground. Communication lines were obliterated, making contacting family members near impossible. When I finally received what little information I could, it was only to learn that my aunt had a stroke, suffering from paralysis on the left side of her body from the neck down. Given that she lives in a medically underserved area, a week and a half passed before she was seen by a physician. She was lucky enough to survive and recover movement, but many thousand others were not. In the immediate aftermath, people continued dying in silence from chronic disease complications or even simple injuries that could have been easily prevented with the appropriate care. As this occurred, I developed an even stronger spirit to fervently pursue my passions towards higher education and training in the field of medicine, hoping to serve my people when I am well-equipped.

While the passing of the hurricane raised awareness in me about the dearth of resources in Puerto Rico, it also made me more conscious about the needs of the underserved population in Boston.

Decidedly so, I became involved in various initiatives in and outside of Harvard. I joined Escalera, a mentoring program focused on underserved youth. Here I had the opportunity to mentor Juan, a 14-year-old high school student displaced by Hurricane María. I was a teaching assistant at HMS MEDscience and its lab-based counterpart HMS MEDscience Lab, with both programs' goals being to introduce students, who came particularly from underrepresented groups, to STEM fields through simulated medical cases. I also had the opportunity to participate in Reflection in Action: Building Healthy Communities, where I offered a workshop to middle-school students from urban areas about mental health and how their social determinants can affect it. Lastly, I along with other Puerto Rican students realized our yearning to contribute to the island and founded the Harvard Puerto Rican Student Association, dedicated to utilizing our diverse trainings and experiences to implement preventive measures for any future disasters. Through all of these initiatives, I have been privileged with the opportunity to better appreciate the importance of a physician's role as a natural attorney for the underprivileged, a role I will take on when I recite my oath.

Here I strive to illustrate what has led me to where I am today: choices. At various moments, I have been faced with choices which ultimately determined the road taken. What I have narrated here are only some of the stories that have gifted me with the grit and resilience I need to achieve my goal of becoming a physician. My passion for the field of medicine originated from the desire to impart in others the sense of reassurance that I felt in my grandmother's care. Through my education, my love of tackling complex challenges, and the choices I made at critical points of my career, I can now honor her impact in me. I strive for a future in which I can influence the systems that enable unnecessary suffering like that which we saw in the wake of catastrophes such as Hurricane María. This will be no easy task; there are many more choices to make. But through it all I will always hold to the memory of that one feeling that began it all: a soothing warmth on my chest and a pervading smell of menthol.

ANALYSIS

Throughout his essay, it is evident that Sergio's Puerto Rican upbringing and identity have played central roles in developing and fueling his passion for medicine and for providing empathetic care to the underprivileged. He writes with nostalgia and emotion as he recalls how his grandmother's care for him when he was a child motivated his desire to become a physician despite the educational obstacles he has had to face. He continues by describing the impact Hurricane Maria and other socioeconomic challenges have had on his understanding of the structural issues that prevent the underprivileged from receiving proper medical care. Through these experiences, he demonstrates clearly that he is driven and dedicated to a career in medicine that will also allow him to give back to his community in Puerto Rico.

Sergio effectively concludes his essay by tying all of the aforementioned stories together under a single theme: choices. He explains how his choices have enabled his experiences and have led him to be the passionate, devoted, and resilient person he is today. In his final sentence, he brings his essay full circle, utilizing the same imagery that he uses to begin his essay. In doing so, Sergio reminds readers that his initial commitment towards providing empathetic care has been and will continue to be fundamental to his aspirations.

—Sabrina Chok

KOBBY A.

Hometown: Stoneham, Massachusetts, USA
Undergraduate and Graduate Schools: Kwame Nkrumah
   University of Science and Technology (Undergraduate).
   University of Massachusetts Lowell (Graduate). Post-
   baccalaureate courses at Harvard Extension School.
Major: Pharmacy/Biological Sciences
GPA: 3.9/4.0 (First Class Honors, WES Evaluated Foreign
   Transcript), 3.9/4.0 (Graduate)
MCAT: 33. PS: 13, V: 9, BS: 11.

ESSAY

My mother was my only parent after my father abandoned us during my childhood in rural Ghana. We scratched out our living by
subsistence farming and relied on homemade concoctions for our
health needs. At eleven years old, I could not imagine that my life
could become any more difficult until one morning when I saw
my mother lying helpless in my uncle's arms as she was rushed out
of our home for a desperate drive to the local clinic. The day before, she had appeared free of her recent episodes of stomach pain.
Now, she had whispered her last words to my older sister. My hope
faded away as I watched her disappear into the distance. That was
the last time I would see my mother alive. In the ensuing days,
my questions about her death would remain unanswered beyond
the fact that she had arrived at the clinic too late to be saved. As
tragic as it was, this experience instilled in me a resolve to find
ways to help curb such loss in my community.

Identity

Fortunately, my oldest aunt became my surrogate mother and gave me a fighting chance to escape the fate that many other orphans faced: ending up on the streets or becoming a victim of child abuse. Inspired by my aunt and teachers, I poured my whole heart into my education and completed high school against the odds of becoming a dropout. By the time I graduated, I had developed a strong interest in science and medicine and was accepted to Kwame Nkrumah University of Science and Technology to study pharmaceutical sciences. In university, I was elected President of the Ghana Pharmaceutical Students' Association amidst shrinking national budgets for community health programs. Still, the impact of poverty forced many rural communities to resort to self-medication with herbal concoctions, antibiotics, or a combination of these to treat their ailments. Realizing how much student efforts could help mitigate this challenge, I initiated projects to raise more than $10,000 to educate rural communities about HIV/AIDS, malaria, and safe use of medications. My interest in medicine grew as I came face-to-face with the grim picture of my nation's healthcare system.

In my senior year of university, I served as a pharmacy intern in a small regional cancer center in Kumasi, Ghana. I also observed medical teams caring for their patients. Like my mother, these patients represented the hopes of many families plagued with the burden of disease and poverty. The folkloric belief that cancer was an irrevocable curse had left some of these patients without hope. Yet, they trusted my naïve advice and agreed to follow their chemotherapy treatment plans. Winning these patients' confidence required both my compassion for them and my respect for their beliefs. Rising above their mythical beliefs, these patients relied upon their connections with the clinic staff for the strength to fight on. However, the glass counter that separated my cubicle from these patients became a literal wall over time; I wanted to connect with them directly to help them in their fight against cancer. These experiences spurred me on my journey to become a physician. I desired to learn about human health and disease so that I could be able to offer help where none existed.

After migrating to the US in 2008, my journey to becoming a doctor took a few detours while I secured my living conditions, supported my family back in Ghana, and eventually, became an American citizen. I undertook graduate studies in biological sciences and internships in medical device R&D at University of Massachusetts Lowell while completing pre-medical courses at the Harvard Extension School. My inspiration to give others a fighting chance also led me to become a non-commissioned officer (NCO) and a combat medic in the U.S. Army Reserve. As a soldier, I took this opportunity to learn medical and non-medical skills to help save the lives of wounded soldiers on the battlefield. I could not be prouder to serve my fellow soldiers and protect the freedoms that make my dreams possible. These dreams now include serving in national and global medical missions. As a volunteer with the Upper Merrimack Valley Medical Reserve Corps (MRC), I serve as an emergency medical technician and assist with local disaster relief operations. With the MRC, I work with community public health programs such as screening patients for hypertension and promoting good health habits at local health fairs. These opportunities to serve in the community have reinforced my resolve to become a physician and work in clinical medicine.

Many people have believed in me, helped me, and given me the hope to overcome my challenges and become what I am today. I believe that I have a duty to give back. The burden of disease and poverty still plague Ghana and other developing countries; hope must prevail in the fight to address this burden.

Identity

I might bring this hope while caring for the sick or wounded. I might pass on knowledge to multiply the available hands in this fight. I might contribute to discoveries that provide new tools to replace disease with health. I must build my capacities first. I look forward to becoming a medical student to nurture myself and ultimately to fulfill this calling.

ANALYSIS

Throughout this essay, Kobby's relentless dedication, even in the face of adversity, to improving the state of health care in his home country of Ghana serves as a glowing display of his character and values.

His essay begins with an impactful moment in his life: his mother's death. Though tragic, it allows Kobby to provide readers with clear insight into why he is so deeply passionate about serving others in his family, community, and country. The story gives the reader a window into what drives him to do what he does.

Kobby then highlights several experiences that have furthered his understanding of the inequalities and issues that permeate Ghana's health care system. With each experience, he shows the reader not only his passion for influencing change in a broken system but also different personal qualities that help paint a more vivid image of his character. Through his descriptions, he demonstrates that he is not only critical and thoughtful but also compassionate and empathetic, ultimately signaling that he has what it takes to be a great doctor.

The conclusion of the essay returns to Kobby's dedication to his home country of Ghana, a theme that is skillfully interwoven throughout the essay. His ability to maintain this consistent theme demonstrates how giving back is always in the back of his mind, motivating him. In his final paragraph, he ruminates about the future and the changes he hopes to bring back to Ghana. In connecting this passion to medical school, he concludes this already strong essay with a convincing case for his determination to become a doctor.

—Owen Searle

GRANT SCHLEIFER

Hometown: Edmond, Oklahoma, USA
Undergraduate School: Private, Emory University
Major: Religion and Biology
GPA: 3.94
MCAT: 526. CP: 132, CARS: 132, BB: 132, PS: 130.

ESSAY

My passion for caring for others began with my mother. Growing up in a working-class family in Oklahoma, my two siblings and I took pride in caring for her. My mother had become quadriplegic years before our births, and opportunities to assist in her care were numerous. Over time, the three of us grew into our various responsibilities, including filling water bottles, emptying leg bags, and transferring my mother from bed to wheelchair and back. That our family could not afford at-home nursing care made our coordinated efforts all the more consequential. Despite our obvious lack of professional training, we understood from experience how to make my mother feel comfortable. When she said "dys," for example, we were not aware of the science behind autonomic dysreflexia but nonetheless knew the steps to relieve the potential causes of her symptoms.

Visits to the neurologist with my mother and subsequent conversations with her about her disability kindled my interest in the nervous system. I diligently cared for my mother but still wondered, "Could there be a cure?" To me, neurology and neurosurgery were salvific powers that might someday allow my mother to carry on like the more able-bodied parents of my friends. This is the context in which I became interested in medicine.

In the summer leading to my senior year of high school, I was granted a scholarship to take two college-level classes at Harvard Summer School. I used this opportunity to explore a topic that, due to my experience as a caregiver, had interested me for ages—neurobiology. Stories by the professor, a physician-researcher in Boston, fed my interest in medicine by humanizing both its practitioners and science. His jokes about the role of the autonomic nervous system in sexual function, in addition to filling the auditorium with laughter, helped destigmatize spinal cord injury. This program allowed me to envision what it might be like to be a doctor and emboldened me to commit to pre-med on my college applications that year.

When I got to college, the relationships I formed with my friend Zoe's parents—both doctors—helped me see how medicine is an art that privileges care just as much as science. Zoe's mother, an internist, was radically perceptive of the needs of her patients, which heightened her ability to make decisions about their care. Her compassionate interactions with patients resonated with my experience taking care of my mother. Throughout college and still today, my continued appreciation for her style of care has validated my sense of calling towards medicine and provided a model I could strive to emulate in my future career.

My work with adolescents with disabilities further shaped my interest in medicine. In my first year out of college, I was a special education co-teacher in D.C. In this role, I collaborated with teachers, families, and social workers to ensure students received their prescribed educational and therapeutic services. Many of these families had appealed to the school system for years to increase their children's access to specialized education, occupational therapy, and other services mandated by federal laws. My job was to help them navigate bureaucratic structures to gain access to these resources.

Three months into my new role in D.C., the issue of disparities in access to public health services took on a new immediacy in my life. One Tuesday at school I learned my mother had unexpectedly passed away. I was shocked and devastated. As I grieved over the following months, I reflected on the significance of my mother's life. I was unsettled that my mother's last months involved her seemingly fruitless struggle with the state welfare system to obtain more than a handful of hours per week of nursing care. Having gone through high school uninsured, I had always felt pangs of injustice at the weakness of our health system to provide for the needs of minors and persons with disabilities. These feelings stimulated my interest in the role of public health in medicine and motivated me to pursue a degree in public health before medical school.

As a public health student, I study how behavioral sciences can be leveraged to reduce health disparities. Currently, I am making forays into sexual minority health by serving as an HIV counselor and providing free HIV testing through a clinical trial on condoms. In addition, I have served as staff supporting the prescribing clinicians in a pilot project to assess the feasibility of prescribing HIV pre-exposure prophylaxis through a telemedicine portal. As a gay man, I have found these experiences incredibly meaningful and hope to continue working in this research area in medical school.

As I use this essay to chart my journey towards medical school, I feel humbled by the people who have enriched my life so far. Their generosity made it possible for someone of my background to attend college and graduate school, which gives me hope and determination to use my education in the service of others. From caring for my mother to advocating for students with disabilities to working in sexual minority health, my experiences inform a unique perspective that will aid in both the study and practice of medicine.

ANALYSIS

Grant's strength lies in his ability to effectively tie together several seemingly different life experiences into a compelling and insightful narrative about his journey to medicine. He details his story chronologically, beginning with his early exposure to medicine through his mother's health issues before bringing readers through his undergraduate and graduate years. However, he doesn't bog readers down with too many details; rather, he strategically selects key moments that not only reveal his multidimensional interest in medicine but also provide readers with insight on his compassionate character.

The final paragraph of this essay is particularly strong. Though it is only three sentences long, Grant succinctly connects his past experiences to a future he envisions in medicine. The distinctive tone the paragraph carries also allows for his humility and his dedication to service and to others to shine through. He leaves readers with a clear sense of his accomplishments and his values and his aspirations and consequently ends with a memorable conclusion to an already strong essay.

—Sabrina Chok

Francisco Ramos

Hometown: San Antonio, Texas, USA
Undergraduate School: Public, The United States Military
  Academy
Major: Environmental Science with Honors
GPA: 3.87
MCAT: 512. CP: 128, CARS: 127, BB: 129, PS: 128.

ESSAY*

My macho Mexican father told me in a serious tone, "Son, you are only allowed to cry once in your life and that time is when your father dies." I was in third grade and I had just witnessed my father cry for the first time at my grandfather's funeral. I do not remember what was said at the services, but rather I remember the 21-gun salute, a military member folding an American flag into a small, perfect triangle and the rows and rows of evenly spaced white tombstones at Fort Sam Houston National Cemetery.

Following my grandfather's death, my father expressed his distrust in the cardiologist's decision to implant a stent into his father's artery. Mr. Vallajo, my grandfather's lifelong neighbor, jokingly told my father, "That's a dead man walking," he had a friend who had died after a stent collapsed. Seven days later my grandfather suffered a massive heart attack. On his last breath he called

---

The views expressed by Mr. Ramos are his own and may not reflect the official policy or position of the Department of the Army, the Department of Defense, or the U.S. Government.

our house and left a harrowing message asking his son, my father, for help. My family did not ask for an autopsy to check if the stent had failed or not, because quite frankly, it would not bring back our loved one. I now question the reasoning for the stent and why not another course of treatment. Perhaps then my grandfather, who I am named after, would have been able to see me swear an oath to the same Constitution he swore an oath to when he joined the United States Army to fight in Korea. However, I am not a physician so I do not have the training, experience, or authority to question that cardiologist's decision, yet.

The second time I saw my father cry was when he unwrapped a Christmas present I had hoped would explain why I wished to serve. The gift was *Photojournalists on War: The Untold Stories from Iraq.* As a Plebe, I flipped through the glossy pages of this collection of images and was spurred to act. I wanted to reach into these photos and wipe the dried blood off an Iraqi child's face. I wanted to lift the Soldier being dragged through the mud off the battlefield. I wanted to cover the burnt bodies lying next to an explosion site. I simply wanted to act. The chaos and inhumanity that I witnessed in these photographs will forever be etched into my soul. I did not see American or Iraqi, Christian or Muslim, nor Soldier or Terrorist. I saw casualties of war who deserved the highest quality of care regardless of their nationality, religion, or affiliation.

I naively joined the Army because I wanted to make a difference in the world. I wanted to right the wrongs I had seen broadcast on the nightly world news. The more I have read and reflected, the more I have come to realize the complex and colossal nature of the issues facing the Middle East and the world. The Army's purpose of maintaining and establishing security will never be solely accomplished by kicking down doors and taking hostages. Violence will not win over the hearts and minds of people who have been subjugated to violence their entire lives. However, genuine care through humanitarian efforts will foster a stronger relationship between the Army and those who oppose us. While at West Point I have been asked how I will balance my duty to the Hippocratic oath to "First, do no harm" and my Oath of Commissioned Officers to "uphold and defend the Constitution of the United States against all enemies, foreign and domestic." I have come to terms with this inner conflict of values by realizing that my role as an Army Physician will be as a noncombatant who treats all casualties of war. I want to deliver the highest quality care to those beyond the veterans like my grandfather, to those photographed individuals in the remote and forgotten corners of the world.

ANALYSIS

Throughout the essay, Francisco aims to show, not tell, the reader that he is a qualified applicant. He successfully accomplishes this by cleverly structuring the essay so that it tells the story of how he realized medicine was for him while also showing the reader he is a good fit for medical school. He captures his curiosity in an anecdote about his grandfather's death, questioning the reason for the medical treatment his grandfather received. He remarks that he does "not have the training, experience, or authority to question that cardiologist's decision, yet," emphasizing that he is intent on pursuing knowledge.

Francisco also demonstrates his caring nature and desire to help people regardless of background, necessary qualities for a good physician, through vivid imagery when he discusses the photography book he gifted his father. He employs repetitive sentence structure, beginning with "I wanted to . . . ," which highlights his eagerness to effect change.

Francisco nicely ties the essay together by explaining how he views his role as an Army Physician, stating that it is the individuals like those in the photographs he desires to care for. This both gives a conclusive ending to the essay and shows his confidence that medical school is the right path for him.

—Katharina Wolf

GREGORY PETERS

Hometown: Bronx, New York, USA
Undergraduate School: Private, College of the Holy Cross
Major: Biological Psychology
GPA: 3.79
MCAT: 33. PS: 12, V: 11, BS: 10.

ESSAY

I envy those whose passions trace back to a perfect anecdote, because mine do not. I did not discover my alma mater by making a wrong turn on the way to another school, I did not meet my girlfriend by sharing an umbrella on a rainy evening, and each time someone asks why I am so determined to study medicine, I provide a different reason. I will share two of my favorites with you.

My housing cooperative, Edgewater Park, is home to a unique cast of characters; picture kids written by Mark Twain from families written by Tennessee Williams. At the center of our enclave in the southeast Bronx stands "the mansion," an old two-story brick building that serves as the home of the Edgewater Park Volunteer Fire Department (EPVFD). I might not have a neat account of how my desire to study medicine originated, but I do have a memory from my time at the EPVFD that serves to remind me why I should persevere through any obstacles in my education and training. While at the scene of a motor vehicle collision we received a call from a man in respiratory distress, forcing us to divide our crew in two. I was seventeen, the youngest of four responders to the latter call, serving as nothing more than a spectator unless something needed to be fetched from the truck. Standing aside dutifully with a stethoscope and blood pressure cuff clenched in my sweaty hands, I watched senior members deliver a few rounds of CPR and then I carried our medical bag back to the truck. On the way I passed by a neighbor who came to claim the dog inside who no longer had an owner. I walked home and looked at the ceiling above my bed for nine hours. I considered quitting the next morning, but decided to sign up for an EMT class instead. Fires and medical emergencies can be scary, but it was that feeling of helplessness that made me question who I am. I resolved to keep my badge and commit myself to earning the trust that comes with it. After all, studying fascinating topics in exchange for knowledge and practical skills that can help people is a small price to pay for a set of eyelids between my eyes and my bedroom ceiling on most nights. This mindset led me to the premedical program at Holy Cross.

In the midst of a dense curriculum of science courses my junior year, I filed away my MCAT materials for later use and became involved in schizophrenia research using a mouse model on campus. That summer I interned on a project using neuroimaging to study executive function in schizophrenia. The following year, I completed a thesis project on clinical and research nosology of schizophrenia as the recipient of the Fenwick Scholar Award. Two years later, I find myself back in the Bronx, sitting in an evaluation room at Einstein listening to a patient describe how this intrusive disorder led him to "give up on life too soon." My three years in neuroscience research have taught me two key lessons about my place in the medical profession. First, I discovered my personal need to diversify my work. I have found that a busy, varied schedule serves to enhance my engagement in each effort I undertake and only enriches the perspective that I carry into it. Plus, it always helps to have exciting results from new data to offset a disturbing firehouse call from the previous night. Second, as much as I love the academic side of medical research and collaborating with fellow lab members, I have learned that having discussions with participants about how our work translates to their lives is my favorite thing in the world to do.

Given the nearly twenty active human research studies at my lab, most of which include a clinical component, I have encountered many people and families with varying degrees of curiosity and concern about the condition that brought them to our lab. As much as I always regretted my very limited ability to help the people to whom I was exposed, I acknowledge the invaluable lesson that it taught me: you rarely help people as much as you hoped or as little as you think. I have administered medical treatment to exactly zero people in my time at the lab, compared to the hundreds of patients I have treated while either volunteering or working as an EMT in New York City. Still, my time spent in dialogue with the family of a child with autism about individualized education programs, or with a participant from the schizophrenia study about how the state of her relationship with her daughter seems to dictate her symptom severity, has gone just as far to convince me that I have chosen the right career to pursue.

While I cannot identify the point in time at which I set my sights on a career in medicine, in retrospect I see a tale of fate at which I cannot help but grin and roll my eyes. Multiple apparently parallel paths that have formed my identity—such as interning in neurosurgery at NYU, serving as a firefighter and EMT in my community, working in a neurophysiology lab at Einstein, and conducting schizophrenia research across multiple disciplines and organizations—seem to serendipitously converge at this application process. Putting my Fenwick thesis into practice, I plan to dedicate myself to the translation of medical research to clinical practice as a whole, and even more to my enjoyment, to the care of my individual patients in the context of their lives.

ANALYSIS

Gregory begins his essay with a clear, honest introduction, in which he admits a lack of a singular source of his passion for medicine. He then briefly lays out the structure of the remaining paragraphs, which gives the essay a clear trajectory and sense of purpose. His candid voice and ability to tell engaging stories with clear takeaways directly related to the medical field make a convincing case for his skills as a future physician.

In the first anecdote, Gregory does not overstate his role in the emergency rescue; rather, he is honest about his helplessness and how it inspired him to learn the skills necessary to assist in such situations. Without stating it outright, Gregory shows the reader that he is humble, honest, and eager to learn. He will do whatever it takes to help others.

In the second anecdote, he describes the two primary lessons that he learned from his neuroscience research. Through these introspective realizations, Gregory convinces the reader that he understands his identity and his purpose. Thus, it becomes clear that he has chosen a fitting career and will be a caring, patient-centric physician.

—Rebecca Lisk

CHRISTOPHER HUENNEKE

Hometown: Cambridge, Massachusetts, USA
Undergraduate School: Public, University of Massachusetts
  Amherst
Major: Biology
GPA: 3.97
MCAT: 516. CP: 129, CARS: 128, BB: 130, PS: 129.

ESSAY

After high school, I chose to join the United States Marine Corps to gain direction and improve my self-efficacy. When I first joined, one of my fears was getting vaccinated. My family raised me to believe that physical disease and sickness were manifestations of incorrect thinking, and that prayer was the only way to treat the sick. Growing up, my mother's epilepsy was ignored and medicine was described as a charlatan's profession. This upbringing instilled in me fear, distrust, and a visceral disdain of all medical professions. When I arrived at Marine Corps Boot Camp, my fellow recruits were terrified of the drill instructors and the upcoming chaos, while I was afraid of the needle. While going through my vaccinations, I realized that many recruits joined the military to gain access to the medical care I was afraid of. During training, I worked hard to overcome my fears and gained confidence that helped in many situations, including dealing with medicine. The very same medical care that relieved my agonizing ingrown toenails and wisdom teeth showed me the importance of medicine firsthand.

During my first deployment to Afghanistan, I participated in an effort to provide healthcare to an isolated community. Many villagers had severe injuries that required immediate medical support. Helping those patients motivated me and filled me with purpose while connecting with them provided new perspectives. After this deployment, I reflected on how my actions helped to bring medical services to a local population, while a year prior I believed those same medical services to be worthless and even harmful. Every action I made had an impact on those around me as well as an impact on myself. I then understood how fortunate I was to have access to medicine whenever it was needed, and how being in a position of advantage requires me to work toward improving the lives of the disadvantaged. In the Marine Corps, I had the privilege of being exposed to many different cultures, hearing the stories of my fellow Marines, and finding common ground despite our different backgrounds. These experiences helped develop me into an effective leader, as I was soon promoted to a platoon sergeant responsible for 60 Marines. Similar to my time in Afghanistan, I found that as a leader I had a dual purpose: physically take care of those in my charge while also providing guidance and support. I learned to have confidence in my decisions, to lead by example, and how to effectively delegate tasks.

These leadership skills were put to work in my personal life through my experiences as a husband and father. Towards the end of my final deployment, my wife and daughter were struck by a drunk driver, resulting in my daughter receiving a severe traumatic brain injury. I was flown home from the Middle East, and while I felt shattered and helpless seeing her on a ventilator, it was reassuring to watch her rapid recovery with the interventions of medical professionals. This desperate need for medicine connected me with the families in those isolated Afghani communities. At that moment, life without medicine was unimaginable, and I experienced what a critical need for medical services felt like. It was hard to believe that just a few years ago, without ever experiencing medical treatment for myself, I had concluded that it was unimportant. Now, I was fortunate enough to have a well-led team of medical professionals in control of my daughter's treatment. My daughter's injury and recovery had changed me, just as my own patient experiences in Marine Corps training had. This experience has inspired me to provide that same reassurance and support to others through a leadership role in medicine. In a few short years I had moved from completely disregarding medicine, to wanting to provide and direct the medical support of those just like my daughter.

My dedication toward medical service has been expressed on multiple fronts. After my daughter's recovery, I reached out to physicians in my military unit and was able to observe their daily routines and gain valuable guidance on the path to becoming a clinician. While in college I researched on the control, function, and development of the nervous system, which will help to further understand neurological diseases and disorders like the epilepsy my mother suffers from. While researching, I grew as a scientist, improved my problem-solving abilities, and gained experience working on a team in an academic environment. Volunteering with the residents of an assisted living facility for veterans has helped keep me connected to the populations that I am a part of, and has given me insight into the role of a clinician.

I will continue to serve others in a capacity that both is relevant to my experiences and will afford me continued development. To me, choosing a career as a leader in medicine is the best way to provide the services I benefited from so richly to all populations of people. By being an empathetic, devoted, and understanding clinician, I want to mentor that young misinformed Marine, my old self, and show him that medical services are not harmful. I want to positively contribute to his values and wellbeing, while providing the leadership that will enable him to come to a positive perspective of medicine.

ANALYSIS

The focus of this essay as a whole is on Christopher's journey of personal growth. Christopher begins by contrasting his fears with the fears of other soldiers he met during his deployment, emphasizing how he had certain values instilled in him throughout his upbringing. This sets him apart from his peers but also establishes the foundations for his personal growth. From that point on, he uses several anecdotes to show his personal journey.

The somber and moving story of his family's car crash is a strength of the essay. Not only does his telling of the story allow the reader to empathize and connect with him, but he is also able to connect the story of the crash back to his experiences in Afghanistan. This places additional and new meaning on the previous stories.

In the conclusion, Christopher is able to concisely state his goals of helping others and developing himself. He also references his "old self." This older version of himself is characterized as a completely different person from who he is today, which further affirms his transformation. Since his time in the military, he has learned so much that he has become a completely new person, but still a person who understands where he comes from. It is clear that he will continue to be committed to personal growth and development, making him an ideal candidate for the medical field.

—Owen Searle

MANUELA VON SNEIDERN

Hometown: Cali, Colombia
Undergraduate School: Private, New York University
Major: Biology and English Literature
GPA: 3.8
MCAT: 514. CP: 128, CARS: 128, BB: 129, PS: 129.

ESSAY

I sat on the second floor of the Centro Médico Dominicano and reassembled, for the fifth time that morning, the plastic eye model I had used to understand the hundreds of ocular disorders introduced in my copy of *The Wills Eye Manual*. Just as I was getting to my favorite part of the assembly process (the lens—how does nature make something so beautifully transparent?), I saw one of Dr. Dauhajre's patients struggling to reach the entrance of the examination room. Jimena was a charming, 82-year-old Colombian woman who had laughed her way through everything life had thrown at her—including nuclear sclerotic cataracts. As I helped Jimena with her walker that morning, however, she remained indifferent, only slightly nodding after I had introduced myself as Dr. Dauhajre's student and asked if I could help her get situated on the exam chair. After several minutes of silence, I noticed a thin band on her left wrist—a bracelet braided with strands of yarn colored yellow, blue and red. I immediately recognized the piece of jewelry; I had seen it countless times in the kiosks of San Andresito, a Colombian shopping center located only miles from my childhood home. "Señora, es usted Colombiana?" I asked. I had never seen a person's countenance soften so suddenly. She tilted her head sideways, smiled, and proceeded to share with me the stories of her grandchildren, her opinions of Colombia's political climate, anecdotes from each of her three marriages, and, most importantly, a passionate discourse regarding the "miracle" of lens replacement, a procedure she hadn't known existed until earlier that week. That same morning, I observed and took notes as Dr. Dauhajre patiently explained the nature of cataract removal surgery. That following Friday, I walked behind Jimena as she was wheeled into the surgery room, and sat next to Dr. Dauhajre and her team as they worked to remove the patient's left lens— no longer transparent, but rather colored with age, wisdom, and character—and replace it with a new multifocal piece that would allow Jimena to perceive the micro expressions on her grandchildren's faces for years to come. I sat next to Jimena in the recovery room, and, as Dr. Dauhajre removed the bandages from the left portion of her face 72 hours later, I witnessed an 82-year-old grandmother get her vision back.

My experience with ophthalmologic surgeons, their teams, and their patients that summer urged me to contextualize myself within the confines of hospital walls. Unlike most surgeons, my exposure to the physicality of the human body had not been through the blade of a scalpel, but rather through the tip of a paintbrush. I grew up an artist. My drawings and paintings have served as a way to express the love I have for my friends and family—when I care for someone, I put them on paper. Over a decade of caring for people and putting them on paper has resulted in countless drawings ranging from my mother's hands to my roommate's knees to a homeless man's brow. I see this aspect of myself reflected in Dr. Dauhajre every time she performs a cataract removal surgery, or, if you will, a redrawing of the human eye. The idiosyncrasies

Identity

of her techniques, the way she dominates both her medium and her tools, and the delicacy with which she approaches her work inspired me to reconsider the boundaries I use to define art. When I care for people, I no longer want to put them on paper. I want to cure them on hospital beds.

The time I've spent at New York University has allowed me to grow not only as an artist, but as a scientist as well. Over the last two and a half years, I've completed several research projects at the Coruzzi Lab, all of which have aimed to investigate nitrogen efficiency in plant roots. This experience has allowed me to reach what I once believed to be an unobtainable level of discipline, as well as a deep appreciation for the value of a structured work ethic. Plants grow—and at the Coruzzi Lab, plants will continue to grow without the slightest regard for me or for my obligations. As a result, I've spent my undergraduate career working and planning around the schedule of a garden weed. At first, the demands of the lab were almost unbearable. Today, they've become an integral, enjoyable, and almost necessary part of my everyday life. After my experience at Retina Associates and Centro Médico Dominicano, I was invited to observe the life of a physician outside the clinical setting; it was during these moments when I realized that medicine requires the same discipline and regimen that have become both a natural part of my daily routine and an indispensable portion of my personal identity.

I believe that my artistic endeavors, research, dedication to the Hispanic community, and medical shadowing experience will one day coexist within hospital rooms. I want to tell someone like Jimena that I will work to restore her health. I want to cooperate with a team to address the health problems of the underserved. I want to redraw the human body. But I must go to medical school first.

ANALYSIS

Manuela begins with an anecdote focused on her interactions with Jimena, a memorable eighty-two-year-old Colombian patient. Her strength is in her elegant prose. She writes vividly, leaving no details unadorned or reflectionless. In doing so, she is able to express convincingly the impact the connection she forged with Jimena that day had in furthering her awe of medicine and her desire to heal others within her community.

She goes on to surprise her readers as she ties her background as an artist to her pursuits to become a doctor. While at first glance the two are seemingly different and almost contradictory paths, as she draws similarities between her careful 2-D depictions of her loved ones and the art of surgery, it becomes obvious that through Manuela's eyes, medicine too can be an art and mimic the expression of care her paintings represented.

Her concise, yet powerful, final paragraph beautifully concludes her essay. Readers are left reminded not only of Jimena, of Manuela's Colombian heritage, and of her love for art and the human body but also of her strong desire to bring multiple facets of her identity to the world of medicine.

—Sabrina Chok

V. INTELLECTUAL DESIRE

AURELIA LEE

Hometown: Brooklyn, New York, USA
Undergraduate School: Public, University of California, Los Angeles
Major: Biomedical Engineering
GPA: 3.95
MCAT: 517. CP: 130, CARS: 127, BB: 130, PS: 130.

ESSAY

It's not every day you help a kid become Iron Man. It happened for me during an internship at the NIH. I was responsible for designing the electronics and software for a portable robotic exoskeleton to help children expressing crouch gait due to cerebral palsy to improve their gait by retraining their muscles and neuron pathways. I saw the project as a fascinating technical problem and immersed myself in solving it.

Then I met Landon. Landon is a child with cerebral palsy expressing crouch gait with limited mobility. When Landon first began training on the robot, he became frustrated. As I watched him become exasperated using the device, it really hit me that I was creating a device for a real person, and the way we delivered his care was every bit as important to what we were doing as delivering an effective technical solution. As his confidence grew, I witnessed Landon, who could barely walk without the device, try to run. We even had to tell him to slow down! He asked if he could bring home the device because it made him feel like Iron Man. This experience crystalized for me my calling, to solve the challenging medical problems children face with love and a deep appreciation for their humanity.

I have firsthand knowledge of what it means to a child with serious medical problems to have loving physicians and nurses. When I was four, I received a heart transplant. Five years later, I fell ill with Hodgkin's Lymphoma. Throughout these difficult and uncertain times, I was fortunate to have a clinical team whose positivity and humor made me feel like a normal kid despite the fact that I was facing grave medical problems. While these experiences were difficult, they gave me a perspective that I treasure because it gives meaning to every day of my life. This perspective is where my calling originates—to become a physician-engineer completely committed to the emotional well-being of each of my patients.

The engineering problems many children face are substantial, and I am grateful for the opportunities I have been given to develop my skills in this area. As a part of my school's design team program I worked on two projects that taught me different aspects of the process of developing medical devices. The first project gave me an overview of the design process of bringing medical devices to market. We developed a neonatal monitoring system for the developing world. We began with a needs assessment and then prototyped our solution to satisfy the specifications we developed. While I focused on the technical development, it was valuable to see other members create a sustainable distribution model because it helped me understand the step by step process by which an idea goes from concept to adoption in the medical field.

For the second project, I was the team leader. On past teams I had a narrow focus on the technical development, but here, I had to be knowledgeable about all aspects of the project and see the big picture in order to develop strategies to move the team forward. I learned how to create contingency plans by reaching out to our numerous advisors in many different specialties to build decision trees.

This project had an extra layer of meaning for me since we were developing an at-home monitoring system for tacrolimus, an immunosuppressant drug I have been taking for over twelve years. Currently, monitoring of this drug's levels can only be done in a clinical setting. Our device allows patients to monitor their levels in the home, allowing for less inconvenience to patients and more data to make more informed clinical decisions.

While my engineering training developed my technical skills, the foundation of my heart and why I will pour myself into my vocation is derived from the love and care I received from my own clinical team as a child. I feel called to be of service to children with serious medical issues, just as my physicians and nurses were to me. One of my favorite volunteer experiences was when I was a camp counselor for Camp Taylor, where I had previously been a camper. Camp Taylor is a week-long camp for children with congenital heart defects designed to create an environment of fun, hope, and normalcy. This is one way in which I can use the difficult experiences of my childhood for good because it is easy for me to bring normalcy to these children's lives since for me, it is normal.

Another volunteer opportunity that has had a tremendous amount of meaning for me is working with the Washington Regional Transplant Community to spread organ donation awareness by telling my story. Since I never received the chance to know my donor family, I use this volunteering as my way to say thank you.

I have enjoyed my engineering studies and my volunteering experiences have been of tremendous value to me, but I cannot wait to go to medical school. It is my desire to be a bridge between the technical engineering world and the direct delivery of care that only physicians can give. I feel it is my mission to use all of my experiences, both good and bad, to find innovative solutions to help the next Wonder Woman and Captain America thrive both physically and in every other part of their lives.

ANALYSIS

What stands out about this essay is how Aurelia hones in specifically on her engineering experiences. Through her references to anecdotes describing her engineering pursuits, such as designing the electronics and software for a portable robotic exoskeleton and working on her school's design team, she is able to showcase all of the unique accomplishments that distinguish her from other applicants. These achievements also provide a testament to her personal character; she elaborates on both her individual contributions as well as the team effort required, indicating that while she is a leader, she also works well in group environments.

Aurelia grounds all of her pursuits in her personal experiences, as she has had her own health complications and has needed certain treatments in order to survive. These health struggles have inspired her to give back by volunteering as a way to say "thank you" to her organ donor. Furthermore, these experiences establish her empathy and show that she has multiple perspectives—the perspectives of both the doctor and the patient.

—Melissa Du

ANGELA CASTELLANOS

Hometown: Orlando, Florida, USA
Undergraduate School: Private, Stanford University
Major: Human Biology
GPA: 3.9
MCAT: n/a

ESSAY

The first time I learned the details of cardiac catheterization, I was translating the procedure in Spanish to a stoic Mexican man in a white Stetson hat. I was the only Spanish interpreter at the Santa Clara Valley Medical Center Emergency Department that afternoon, so it was up to me to understand and relay the details of the procedure from the cardiologist to the patient and her husband—hat now in hand. I fumbled over the words, attempting at once to convey and comprehend the thought of a guide wire traveling from her short, bruised leg up to her heart. After a few minutes of silence, her husband, unblinking, finally said, "Si," and the team whisked his wife away.

After the commotion had subsided, the man walked over to me and he shook my hand with both of his own. "Gracias, Doctora," he said softly from under his wide brim, walking away before I could correct him.

As a child growing up in suburban Central Florida, my experience with medicine was limited to the occasional 10-minute checkup with my family doctor. However, as I spent time in the Santa Clara emergency room, medicine became a window not just into the health but also into the fears and the values of a community. After my experience with the man in the white Stetson hat and many others like him, I saw in medicine the dynamic intersection of cutting-edge science and a community at their most vulnerable.

I have always been fascinated by stories that expand my personal definition of what it means to be human, stories that challenge my ideas of success, of suffering and of happiness. While I have found that medicine fulfills my desire to find and contribute to such stories, my interest initially led me to study journalism at the University of Florida. In search of a story and hoping to continue the international service work I did in high school, I joined a service organization in college and took a trip to the rural Atlantic coast of Nicaragua. While in Puerto Cabezas, our group toured a local hospital filled with post-operative hammocks hanging in the muggy air. Instead of taking notes for a potential article, I spent my day teaching a young girl who was recovering from an appendectomy how to draw.

My ambition to serve others is rooted in my upbringing. My parents came to the United States from Colombia in the 1980s and raised two children while completing undergraduate and master's degrees. Just as they instilled the value of education in me, my parents also showed me the value of community by opening our home to other newly arriving Colombian families and by funding an orphanage in Bogotá, Colombia, upon reaching financial stability. They model a combination of compassion and work ethic that I strive for daily.

My junior year, I transferred to Stanford University to refocus my fascination with human behavior and stories. As a Human Biology major, I immersed myself in the neural and molecular mechanisms of behavior as well as the broader fields of international health and medical humanities. Human Biology introduced me to a medicine that valued patients' stories as much as rigorous scientific research.

During my year as a Spanish emergency department interpreter, I was just as intrigued by the atmosphere of the hospital as I was by the details of the diagnoses. I expected the doctors to be knowledgeable, but they also displayed a surprising level of empathy and humility. I watched an intern comfort a tearful woman as she inspected her products of conception after a spontaneous abortion. I observed a doctor mediate a tense discussion between a desperate man with wide gashes on his wrists and his horrified family. While I facilitated dozens of pelvic exams, the individual nature of each patient's worries made the exams anything but monotonous. These 8-hour shifts were filled with more stories than I had experienced in my whole summer as a journalist.

After graduation, I joined the Cognitive Neuroscience Laboratory at Harvard University as a research assistant. I was eager to explore the mysterious relationship between brain and behavior while learning to think like a scientist and design my own experiments. Marco, an undergraduate student whom I have been mentoring in the lab, asked me why we are collecting DNA samples for a genome-wide association study and why we are analyzing cerebellar topography. In answering his questions and the questions of the hundreds of participants I've scanned as part of our MRI studies, I have realized that I want to be a physician because I want to help personalize the implications of the often-inaccessible world of research. I want to help people navigate through the biological, emotional and existential questions of medical science.

I have spent my life trying to understand people through their stories and through science. In medicine, I have found the depth of knowledge I crave from science, coupled with the sense of community I value from my journalism experience and upbringing. Few careers offer intense intellectual challenges alongside humbling, personal interactions with other members of the community. A life in medicine will allow me to learn about the human body in the service of the human condition, and I hope to strengthen that connection throughout my career for myself and for others.

ANALYSIS

Angela begins with a powerful and impressive introduction: she retells a scene in which she used her language abilities to help a patient understand her treatment, unintimidated by the stoicity of the husband and the pressure to convey the information accurately. Tactful descriptions of the moment, from the "unblinking" husband to the operations team having "whisked" the patient away, make palpable the intensity of the situation. So when in the end the husband unexpectedly thanks Angela and mistakenly calls her a *doctor*, we see that she has rendered a service that was helpful and professional to such an extent that it led her to being recognized as a doctor.

Angela segues from this intro into an overview of how medicine has constantly been in contact with her life since her early childhood, particularly in the aspect of connecting to and helping people. In particular, she potently relates a seemingly tangential interest in journalism to her deeper motivation to understand the human experience; in particular, she notes how she traveled in search of a story but found instead an opportunity to care for a recovering patient. From there, the scenes she describes, from her parents' compassion to her experiences and observations while working in the emergency department, illustrate how her life path has fortified her appreciation for the human condition and her drive to, like from the introduction, make medicine accessible to others.

—George Moe

JENNIFER CHOI

Hometown: Spokane, Washington, USA
Undergraduate School: Private, University of Washington
Major: Bioengineering
GPA: 3.81
MCAT: 35. PS: 12, V: 11, BS: 12.

ESSAY

I stood nervously among a sea of bodies in the chilly pre-dawn glow. My impulsive idea to run the 2013 Seattle Marathon was finally coming to fruition. Surging forward at the sound of the gun, it didn't take long to settle into the familiar rhythm of all those early morning runs around Lake Washington. My love of running is not the result of winning races; instead, it is the product of a long process of discovering the euphoria that can be found in personal improvement, challenging oneself, and the freedom of being in the outdoors. I love the incremental challenges of pressing forward, the striving for constant progress toward a goal. In a similar fashion, my initial interest in medicine has manifested into a passion as I have explored the field during my undergraduate years.

My first steps into the medical field began with my fascination with the pathophysiology and treatment of diseases, which motivated me to study bioengineering. As a bioengineering major, I sought to design and build new solutions to address medical problems and impact others through research. In particular, I became involved in the development of gene therapies because of their potential to cure a plethora of diseases, many of which currently do not have satisfactory treatment options. In an effort to overcome many of the barriers to efficient gene delivery, we sought to design nonviral vectors with multiple functionalities. As a result of my research in Dr. Suzie Pun's lab, we elucidated novel design criteria for developing cationic copolymers for gene delivery, ranging from polymer architecture to hydrodynamic morphology.

Although I was inspired by the theoretical potential of gene therapy, I also witnessed the personal, patient-level impact of bioengineering innovations. As a volunteer in Uganda, I used Hema-Strip HIV Test strips to identify patients who needed life-saving antiretroviral therapy. Even in relatively unskilled hands, this product of modern bioengineering enabled rapid, cost-effective, and reliable patient diagnoses. As a doctor, my bioengineering and research background will provide me a unique toolset that will help me propel the medical field towards treating and curing more patients.

Providing excellent patient care is the first priority for any physician, but mentoring and teaching are also equally important for ensuring a high standard of care. As co-founder of the bioengineering department's first undergraduate journal club, which aimed to create a comfortable and mentally stimulating environment for students to learn how to approach scientific literature, I was able to actively participate in helping fellow students grow as future researchers. I found a similar kind of fulfillment as a youth group leader at my church. When a high school student reached out to me about her struggles with depression and self-harm, I did my best to give her the friendship and care she desperately needed. Coffee dates and late-night Facebook chats became routine for us. Through this process, I watched her transform from timid and distant to vibrant, smiling, and social. A year later, she is involved in activities like tennis and is actively rebuilding her relationship with her parents. The immense satisfaction found in mentoring others and seeing them improve and advance motivates me to seek out opportunities to continue mentoring as part of a career in academic medicine.

Shadowing my own mentor, Dr. Joo Ha Hwang, solidified my dreams of pursuing a career in academic medicine. Through my time with him, I was ecstatic to find that my passions for medicine, research, and mentoring were all an integral part of Dr. Hwang's everyday job. Not only does he practice medicine, he also runs his own research group and develops novel therapies and diagnostics that utilize endoscopy. As his medical students and residents were preparing to go out on consults, Dr. Hwang provided the guidance and advice they needed. Even when they were worn from the challenges they faced, he remained encouraging and supportive. Likewise, his interactions with patients and their families reminded me of the personal connections fundamental to being a doctor. When communicating with the family of a patient dying of chronic liver failure, I was humbled by his ability to deliver the realities of the situation with compassion and sympathy. Although he didn't sugar-coat anything, even I, a total stranger to the patient, felt comforted and reassured by his words. The potential to impact others on a personal level, as well as indirectly through advancements in medicine, inspires me as I embark on the journey to academic medicine.

As my blood-stained shoes finally passed the marathon finish line, the exhilaration cancelled out the screaming agony of my body. Looking at the clock, I realized I had run a Boston qualifying time. Losing a few toenails and many hours of sleep is a minor sacrifice on a journey of discovery and improvement. My commitment to the various aspects of medicine will also be fruitful. Through my undergraduate experiences in research, teaching, and service, my passions for scientific inquiry, novel thinking, patient care, and helping others have solidified my commitment to pursuing a career with local and global impacts in academic medicine.

ANALYSIS

Jennifer opens her essay with her experience running the Seattle Marathon. She loves running not because she likes to win races, but because she is drawn to the process of challenging herself and becoming the best version of herself that she can be. These values that she defines in the context of running she then extends to medicine, which highlights how she will thrive in an environment that is similarly physically and mentally demanding.

Jennifer then delves into her experiences mentoring others, doing research, and co-founding the undergraduate journal club. Through all of these examples, she illustrates her strengths as a leader and a critical thinker. The anecdote in the fourth paragraph not only puts further emphasis on her great mentorship skills but also attests to her passion to impact people on a personal level.

When Jennifer goes in depth about shadowing her own mentor, the reader sees how she truly values being a student as well as a teacher. She admires Dr. Hwang's empathy and confidence and aspires to exhibit these characteristics when she becomes a physician. This shows the reader that she is excited to commit herself to the medical field, just as she has committed herself to self-improvement through running.

—Evelyn Manyatta

KATE KOCH

Hometown: Cleveland, Ohio, USA
Undergraduate School: Private, Massachusetts Institute of
  Technology
Major: Biology
GPA: 5.0
MCAT: 34. PS: 10, V: 11, BS: 13.

ESSAY

I have always loved a challenge, whether it has been conducting scientific research since age 15, volunteering on Massachusetts General Hospital's (MGH's) chemotherapy unit, stepping on the ice as the first woman to play men's hockey at MIT or teaching genetics as an undergraduate teaching assistant (TA) with a team of graduate TAs. My experiences have resulted in an excitement for tackling challenges and a passion for problem solving. One MIT president put it best when he compared getting an education from MIT to drinking from a fire hose. I view the practice of medicine and the care of patients in much the same way. I am drawn to medicine because it is a dynamic field filled with new challenges. I have seen that the challenges in patient care become particularly complex because of the need to consider both the treatment of the disease and the individual. I am inspired and motivated to pursue an MD because I want to engage myself in the challenge of treating the patient.

From an early age through high school I was encouraged to embrace my school's motto "we learn not for school but for life."

Intellectual Desire

Cultivating this attitude has helped me to excel and develop a love for learning. Applying this philosophy at MIT, I have developed a passion for biology and medically related research especially within the field of cancer. From my research, especially at MIT and the Cleveland Clinic, I have come to realize that medicine is a constantly evolving field, and that physicians are frequently presented with new obstacles or discoveries that may change the way in which medicine is practiced. Thus, they must adapt and always be willing to learn. Conducting research in various labs over the past 6 years, I have learned how to adapt by combining and applying concepts from my curriculum and past lab and hospital experiences to the project at hand. A career in medicine is an opportunity to continue "learning for life," as I attempt to solve various problems presented by patients. I look forward to investigating the unanswered questions in medicine and applying solutions to patient care. As a physician, I want to use my medical knowledge and understanding of the patient to create better outcomes for my patients and others.

Beyond problem solving and "learning for life," developing relationships with patients is a central part of being a physician. With two physician parents, I have spent a lot of time observing the development of these relationships. My father is a cardiologist, and watching how patients greet him in and outside the hospital, thank him with tears in their eyes or claim that they would not be alive today if it were not for him makes me realize the importance of relationships and inspires me to pursue an MD. What makes him a great physician is his effort to get to know each patient as a person. As an MGH volunteer, I have had the privilege of a similar experience. I learned firsthand that treating a patient goes beyond administering medication—it is about connecting with the patient as a person. I volunteered on the chemotherapy infusion unit, serving lunch to patients and talking with them. Studying cancer in my classes and in lab did not prepare me for my first day. At the cellular level cancer is a terrible disease, but I discovered that at the clinical level it can be devastating to more than just the body. Over time, I developed my own relationships with the patients I saw each week and, while I was not administering treatment, I realized that I was still able to provide a crucial component of care. I came to see that patient care calls on physicians to not simply define patients by their disease, but as unique individuals in need of a human connection, which I was able to provide. The sincere thanks I received after something as simple as a conversation or getting a patient to smile illustrated how much these connections were appreciated. As a volunteer, I could only help in treating the person, but as a physician, I can give more. I want an MD because I want to give more. I want to be able to treat the individual and the disease.

From spending time at MGH, Cleveland Clinic and other hospitals, I have seen that great physicians possess certain qualities. Medicine is a group effort and great physicians are "team players," something with which I am very familiar. Over the past 16 years, ice hockey has taught me to value discipline, persistence, focus, and keeping my cool. Great physicians must also embody these qualities. In addition, they are good teachers and effective communicators who can connect with patients from different backgrounds and with different levels of understanding. As a TA for genetics, I had to develop a similar skill set in order to communicate concepts in a number of ways so that different students could understand. Ultimately, my experiences in research, at MGH, at MIT and even on the ice have shaped me into a team player, a leader, a teacher, a perpetual student, a scientist and a problem solver with a love for challenges. Because of my experiences, I aspire to engage in the challenge of treating patients because, while it can be difficult, I have seen that the reward is always greater than the challenge.

ANALYSIS

The concept of relishing challenges is used time and time again by students—however, Kate's essay stands out because of the narratives she weaves into the essay. In the examples that she provides, she demonstrates that she is a leader and pioneer by listing unique experiences and characteristics that distinguish herself from other applicants. Thus, she immediately hooks the reader in and leaves the reader eager to learn more about her story.

Kate's strength also lies in the structure of her essay. She uses overarching themes, such as a love for challenges and the philosophy "we learn not for school but for life," to build upon her relationship with medicine and explain how her values align with being a physician.

Finally, Kate clearly communicates how her different life experiences have shaped her character. She cites experiences that range from her athletic to her academic to her medical pursuits, giving the reader a sense of how well-rounded she is. Thus, she makes it clear that she will thrive in a medical environment when interacting with patients, doctors, and peers.

—Melissa Du

J. C. PANAGIDES

Hometown: Sterling, Virginia, USA
Undergraduate School: Public, University of Virginia
Major: Biomedical Engineering, Applied Mathematics
GPA: 3.9
MCAT: n/a

ESSAY

While not a scientific endeavor, allowing Google to auto-populate queries into an empty search bar is an amusing way to glimpse at the most pressing medical needs of our modern America. In response to the incomplete search "why does my . . . ," Google interrupts to complete the question: ". . . stomach hurt? . . . chest hurt? . . . back hurt? . . . head hurt? . . . cat lick me?" before listing a diaspora of more specific inquiries such as "why does my nose sweat?" and perhaps the more creative "what would a chair look like if your knees bent the other way?" Clearly, the search bar is a place for personalized medicine and furniture visionaries alike.

Despite its peculiarities, the Google algorithm may be on to something. The top five auto-complete suggestions for "why does my . . ." (listed above) remarkably include 3 out of the 4 most common chief complaints reported during ER visits at Beth Israel in Boston, MA. Only shortness of breath is missing from the list. Such a striking comparison prompts thorough evaluation of the following hypotheses: 1) people with acute SOB know to seek medical attention in hospitals in lieu of Google, and 2) people who have seemingly any other type of pain would prefer the first opinion of WebMD.

Intellectual Desire

Unfortunately, not all public opinions are so innocuous. The search "doctors are . . ." reveals disturbing attitudes toward physicians, suggesting predicates "useless, evil, overpaid, arrogant." Surgeons do not fare much better, with the auto-filled adjectives "jerks, crazy, weird." Yet not all medical professionals face the same criticism. By similar search methodology, nurses are "us, angels, awesome, heroes." Such incongruity was examined in a 2017 PLOS study (Ref 1) which found greater declines in explicit empathy in medical students throughout their training compared to students of nursing and related fields. However, these results contradict the findings of a 2016 NPR poll which revealed that a clear majority (80%) of respondents described their personal medical care as "good" or "excellent." What could explain this discrepancy?

Subjective attitudes are notoriously difficult to characterize, even with carefully constructed methodologies. On a superficial level, my undergraduate engineering education may seem to encourage the algorithmic performance-based analyses that contribute to an over-reliance on the technical aspects of medicine and perhaps devalue marginalized voices. However, this cannot be farther from the truth. Just like medicine, the practice of engineering is maintained in a continual cycle of re-invention, wholly characterized by the interactions between provider, client, and environment. My experience optimizing ceramic water filter production in South Africa taught me that the best solutions are often derived from careful listening in an effort to assess fundamental challenges. So when an exasperated patient in the ER explains that she's already been asked "what brought you to the ED this evening?" five times before a physician even made contact with her, I see not an institutional shortcoming but an opportunity to optimize a human process for the sake of the user.

Medical journalism offers a window into the inner workings

of the modern medical machine from a variety of perspectives including both patient and provider. In particular, I admire the candid writings of American surgeon Atul Gawande. In his 2014 novel *Being Mortal*, Gawande proposes that the ultimate goal of engaging with a career in medicine is masterful competency. I agree with Gawande's view that competency itself creates a sense of identity for the medical profession. However, he notes there is thus no larger threat to a physician's sense of identity than a patient who is "unfixable" (of which nature provides plenty). To its merit, the pursuit of deep competency in medicine has contributed to the discoveries that have markedly improved the average quality of life throughout human history, and my experiences working on the front lines of medicine as an EMT and medical scribe have reinforced in my mind the value of quality medical interventionism. However, I believe that the idea of complete mastery refracts what doctors are capable of into what the public now expects of modern medicine, creating tensions on both sides of the patient-provider dichotomy. I would like to become a physician to realize the potential of empathetic medicine to revolutionize how medical care is administered and ultimately help patients maintain a greater sense of autonomy both in the nuances of daily living and the challenges at the end of life.

It is true that the institutions of medicine are well-established, and healthcare is a complex network complete with thousands of regulatory clusters and millions of individual nodes that deserve the benefit of time-forged respect. Yet if there is one thing I wish to contribute during my nascent entry into medicine, it is that the life of ideas does not yield to eternal pedagogical rigidity. Instead, medicine glimpses into the life of individuals who offer opportunities to reinvent healthcare and suggest incremental steps toward even a well-tempered mastery.

Intellectual Desire

(1) http://journals.plos.org/plosone/article?id=10.1371/journal.pone .0183352

ANALYSIS

J.C. begins with a witty introduction that immediately captures his readers' attention. His topic of choice, Google searches, might initially seem mundane, but it quickly becomes relatable and enables his curious and humorous personality to shine through. As he continues to carefully present information and questions for readers to consider, he gives readers a glimpse into the way he thinks and demonstrates that he is both analytical and critical of the current state of health care and medical institutions.

Despite the essay's focus on his intellectual curiosities, J.C. strikes an effective balance between writing about ideas that fascinate him and his own experiences. For instance, he elegantly connects his background in engineering to medicine, drawing parallels between the value of reinvention in both fields. He also applies key learnings from his international experiences in South Africa to better understand his interactions with patients in the ER. This strategic placement of relevant experiences effectively allows him to not only contextualize why particular ideas in medicine interest him but also to showcase the variety of work he has done.

These experiences and ideas effectively build up to the strong declaration in J.C.'s concluding paragraphs. They serve as a fitting backdrop as he makes a convincing and memorable case for how he hopes to contribute to medicine.

—Sabrina Chok

APPLICANT ADVICE

ON PREPARATION

Azucena Ramos: "Try not to compare yourself to other premed students out there. You are unique and so is your journey to medicine. Embrace that and use it to your advantage. The thing that is going to set you apart from everyone else is your ability to tell your story in a compelling way. You should spend a significant amount of time reflecting on why you want to be a doctor and try to distill that down into an easy-to-digest but powerful personal statement. In the end, your personal statement should accomplish the following: 1. It needs to answer the question, "Why do you want to be a doctor?" 2. It needs to tell a powerful, memorable story that tells admissions more about you as an applicant, and 3. It needs to convey your passion for the medical field. Medical training is long and arduous, and schools want to make sure they select people who are ready for the long haul."

Grant Schleifer: "Take your time studying for the MCAT and applying to medical school. There is nothing shameful about taking multiple gap years to feel ready for medical school."

Nina Allen: "Don't focus on the scores or the GPAs. It's all just a small part of what matters. Focus on you and doing things that excite you, push you out of your comfort zone, and help you develop/evolve as a person. Don't try to be the perfect premed, it's all an illusion. Just be you, do things that are meaningful to you.

The right medical school(s) for you will uplift and empower you to do those things, too, and the other ones just aren't worth your time anyways."

Christopher Huenneke: "Be persistent, put your max effort into all your activities, and never give up. Be concise and truthful in your narrative. Take time to plan your timeline appropriately and stick to it!"

Kyle R. B.: "During the interview process, have confidence in yourself and be your own biggest advocate! You may feel doubtful about whether or not your achievements hold a flame to the torches of others. However, if you are unable to take pride in your performance, it will be more challenging convincing others that your assets hold great value. Find mentorship in those who have come before you, and don't be reluctant to ask for help! Everyone who you aspire to be has, at some point in their lives, experienced the challenges that you will overcome!"

Zachary Johannesson: "Be open and honest about what drives your desire to pursue health care. Don't just write what you think the admissions boards want to hear."

ON BEING YOURSELF

Agatha Brzezinski: "Be yourself! As a premedical student, I always found myself asking what admissions committees would think of the activities I was signing up for and how I was choosing to spend my time. However, in the two years before I applied, I decided to spend my time the way I wanted to, which meant completely throwing myself into studying foreign languages. Ultimately, I tied this passion into patient care during my interviews and found it well received. The truth is that we need doctors of all types with diverse interests and passions. Figure out who you are, what you love, and what drives you and let that shine through as you apply to medical school! Good luck!"

Gabriel Molina: "Never minimize the passions and hobbies that make you unique, even—and especially—when, on the surface, they may have little to do with medicine. These are the pieces of your application—and personality—that will ensure you succeed in medical school and beyond."

Hazel W.: "Be genuine. Whatever your experiences have been, directly relevant to medicine or otherwise, be true to them. Don't exaggerate who you are or what you've been through, instead, use your application to give schools an honest look at who you are, what you value, and what draws you to medicine. In the same vein, as you go through college and any years you may have been graduating and applying, do the things you genuinely feel a desire to do, not things you feel required to do to check a box. You'll be surprised by how well your experiences can be woven into a compelling personal narrative that appeals to a medical school admissions committee."

Kobby A.: "You may realize from my very nontraditional background that the road to medical school is not necessarily a 'one-size-fits-all.' My biggest advice is to know and be your best self. First, remember that your journey is quite unique from many others', true of both traditional and nontraditional applicants. Your biggest task is to capture and show this uniqueness (academics, services/volunteer, research, or other extracurricular commitments/interests) in your application. Your biggest challenge is to balance this self-awareness and confidence with humility, knowing that other applicants have unique journeys, too. After all, they are your potential future colleagues, and it is worth realizing and celebrating their uniqueness for the ultimate benefit of your patients and the medical profession at large. So, I hope you find the confidence from your unquietness to humbly 'customize' it into all aspects of the application. Good luck!"

THE HARVARD CRIMSON has been the daily newspaper of Harvard University since 1873. It is the nation's oldest continually operating daily college newspaper.